God's Blueprint for a Happy Home

God's Blueprint for a Happy Home

by
Lester Sumrall

New Leaf Press

ISBN: 0-89221-251-9
Library of Congress Catalog: 93-87259

Dedication

*This book
is dedicated
to Louise Sumrall.
We knew each other for
almost 52 years, and we lived
together as husband and wife 49 years
and 8 months before she went to
heaven. Her husband, her sons,
and her family all love her
memory, and together
we dedicate
this book.*

Contents

Introduction

The popular television show of the 1950s, "Leave It to Beaver," featured the comical escapades of a young boy, his brother, and their parents. Ward and June Cleaver raised their sons to respect authority and to have integrity. Every day after school, the boys would enter the house through the kitchen, grab a glass of milk and a few cookies, and actually have a conversation with their mother. When dad came home from work, they all sat together around the dining room table, enjoying an evening meal and lively conversation.

Today, the syndicated reruns of this program generate laughter from viewers, but not because of the comedy elements of the stories. Instead, it is popular to make fun of the traditional values a fictional family like the Cleavers espoused. Today the image of a God-fearing family is mocked.

We know the carefree days depicted on those

long-ago television shows didn't always exist. Even in the 1950s, family conflicts were inevitable. Still, parents and children knew their respective roles, resulting in a sense of security and stability that allowed them to function and live together happily. Parents took the time to train and discipline their children who were taught to say, "Yes, sir" and "Yes, ma'am."

The modern picture of a family, however, is much different from what some of us call the "good old days."

In the 1990s, television sitcoms portray even young children as wise-cracking smart alecks who zing their parents with demeaning phrases while the studio audience roars with laughter. In most cases, Mom is an accomplished career woman who, of course, is smarter than her husband — if she has one — and Dad appears to be an oaf undeserving of respect.

The networks want us to believe that "normal" is a home where two mothers — or two bachelors — are raising their children together. Or where a widowed father lives with his own three children, his brother-in-law, and his best friend or maybe a cousin or a housekeeper— all in the same house!

Like "Leave It to Beaver" in times past, all TV conflicts today are resolved in less than half an hour, and every program ends with a smile and a hug. Television sitcoms will never portray real life because real life for many families involves constant arguing and quarreling that is *never* resolved.

In many families, relationships are strained

or broken by bitterness and unforgiveness. Commitment and respect for one another have been replaced by disloyalty and cynicism. Trust and integrity are non-existent as family members lie and deceive to get their own way.

In many families, there is no chain of command or line of authority now that children are encouraged to demand their "rights" and considered equal to their parents. Even humor within the family has been reduced to put-downs and snide remarks that destroy self-esteem and create a constant atmosphere of hostility.

No wonder divorce is rampant, and children are displaced, bouncing from Mom's house to Dad's place with no sense of security.

This kind of arrangement affects children in different ways. A boy who loses his father in a divorce becomes bitter and rebels. He sees his father once a month when what he really needs is his neck hugged and a game of catch each evening. The mother — now a single mom — does her best, but she has to maintain the house, work outside the home, and juggle the finances. Left to fend for himself for hours at a time, the child flounders without adult supervision or parental guidance.

What ever happened to the image of a happy home? Is one even possible in today's world? Reality does suggest that, in our society, the harmonious, two-parent family united by the Holy Spirit is a rare treasure indeed. But it is not impossible.

Like building a house, developing a happy home requires a plan — a blueprint — that outlines where every component should be placed in order to have a solid structure.

Where do we go to find the blueprint for a properly functioning family? We must go to the Source — to the Builder who created marriage and the family.

When you observe a giant skyscraper standing stately and tall, do you muse to your children that it is just a natural phenomenon that evolved without any planning?

No, that would be foolish.

That architectural masterpiece was created piece by piece by master craftsmen and checked by the most scrutinizing of inspectors so that it can withstand the brutal forces of nature without toppling.

Likewise, when you see a man and woman and their children in a very happy home, it is not an accident. It did not *just happen.*

You have to *make* a happy home. It doesn't just fall into place. If you don't understand the ingredients of a strong and happy home, then you will never have one.

In the chapters that follow, we will look at the components necessary to construct and maintain a solid family structure that will not collapse under the pressures of the stressful world in which we live.

Like a house, the maintenance of a solid family requires hard labor and constant diligence, but the rewards — both in this life and in the blessed one to come — are much greater than the alternative.

It is my sincere desire that this book will help you enjoy a happy family life and keep your family strong and secure in the days to come.

Marriage: Foundation for the Family

*Therefore a man shall leave his
father and mother and be joined to
his wife, and they shall become one
flesh.* — Genesis 2:24:NKJ

A respected pastor and his lovely wife recently came to me for counseling.

They smiled and shook hands with my staff, but as soon as my office door closed, their masks came off. Although he is the minister of one of the finest congregations in America and she is a respected Christian educator, they began acting more heathen than some of the most pagan, demon-worshipping tribesmen I have preached to in equatorial jungles.

"I just want to be alone and not have her around anymore," he whined. "She's been hurting me for the last eight or nine years, telling our young children that they don't need to obey my discipline."

She responded in angry tears that she was "tired of never being told I am loved, never being appreciated, and always being ordered around by a brooding dictator who is convinced that the entire world should cringe at the sound of his bark."

He shot back that "she never kisses me; she never loves me; she is too busy with her work."

She spat that he had "no respect for my career" and that she was "tired of being demeaned" and sick of worrying whether he was going to be threatened by her success.

"He takes it out on the children, lording it over them as if somebody died and made him king," she complained. "I am so sick of his standing up there in his high and mighty pulpit, pretending to have all the answers for the whole world, when he can't even make his own children love him."

For several hours, I heard them spew ugliness at each other. It was awful. Here were two Christian leaders — symbolizing the forces that hold together our civilization. One led a highly respected church. The other is training our next generation.

They were married, but the flame of their love was flickering as each of them hardened their heart against the other.

What was missing? The answer lies in their

expectations of marriage and why they got married in the first place. Many people get married for the wrong reasons.

Three Ways to Get Married

There are three ways to get married.

In America, most people get married by a union of the flesh. In other words, their relationship is based on lust. That is why there are so many divorces. Lust of the flesh is not a strong enough foundation to support a marriage and keep a husband and wife together.

The second group gets married because they feel a unity of their souls or minds. How does this happen?

A young man going to college meets a female student, and they talk together.

He says, "Hey, she thinks like I think." Their minds have found a common bond.

Then they play tennis together, and he thinks, *Hey, she likes the same things I do.* Their souls enjoy the same pleasures.

"Her emotions are similar to my emotions. I like the way she responds to the issues of life. Isn't that amazing? When she makes a decision, I like it!" Their souls are in agreement — at least at this point in their lives — so they get married.

The trivial likes and dislikes that initially drew them together, however, do not form a solid framework for their marriage. Why? Because likes and dislikes change. As a result, he grows one way and she grows another way, and they don't function in unity of soul like they did before. They don't see things exactly the same anymore. Their cardboard marriage begins to deteriorate, and with nothing substantial to hold it together, they divorce.

The third way to get married is by a uniting of the spirit. This can only take place between two believing Christians who are born again by the Spirit of God. That's why the Bible says, "Do not be yoked together with unbelievers" (2 Cor. 6:14).

When I first met the young woman who would later become my wife, I didn't know much about her. My flesh, however, told me she was beautiful, and as we talked, I learned that we had many soulish things in common.

What drew me to Louise most, however, was her obvious and tested commitment to serving Christ at any cost. As a missionary in Argentina, she had given her life to reaching the lost in the far corners of the earth.

I said to myself, *She would make a suitable wife for me. I am a missionary, and Louise is already a missionary. I think that the Lord would like for us to team up and do our Christian spiritual work together.*

For two years, we corresponded by mail since my missionary travels at the time took me to many places around the world. When I received Louise's letter accepting my proposal of marriage, I made this entry in my journal that day: "May God unite our lives to do a great work for Him in every part of the world."

God prepared her for my life and prepared

me to be her husband. I found great joy, peace, and fulfillment in my unity with this devoted woman of God. Louise and I were one in spirit, and every day, I thank the Lord for sending her to me.

In almost 50 years of marriage, we did not have a serious quarrel and enjoyed a beautiful life. The word "divorce" was never spoken in our house unless we were talking about someone for whom we needed to pray.

Now that she has gone to be with the Lord in heaven, I miss her terribly. A part of me has been taken away.

Our lives were so intertwined that we preferred being with one another over anyone else. When working in my office at home, I would often look up to find Louise quietly sitting across from my desk.

When I would ask, "Do you need to talk to me about something?" she would invariably reply, "No, I just wanted to be with you."

If I got up and went to do something in the front room, pretty soon I would find she had followed me there also. Louise and I were companions in the deepest sense of the word.

Those who get married in the spirit find that the needs of the soul and flesh are also wonderfully met. The mind finds common ground for growth, and the flesh enjoys satisfaction that transcends time and age. All three aspects of the human nature flow together in a unity that makes the man and wife one.

And that is what marriage is all about.

Whose Idea Was It?

The mystery of marriage — the uniting of one man and one woman — originated in the Garden of Eden. By mystery, I mean the inexplicable, impossible idea that two people can become one person.

Like a wedding band on the finger of a man and a woman, their relationship forms a circle. In marriage, a husband and wife are united until one of them dies. Their covenant is for the full cycle of a life not just for a season.

Marriage was instituted by God himself; it was not man's idea.

God, who had just spoken the stars and the sun into existence and planted the Garden of Eden with its exquisite beauty, also conceived the idea of a man and a women becoming one.

The Almighty decided to create Adam by himself at first as a solitary being. I wonder if perhaps God did this so Adam could experience how it feels to be all alone in the world. That way Adam would more deeply appreciate the gift of having another human being to share his life.

Although the Garden of Eden was filled with beauty, the Bible says that Adam had a profound emptiness in his heart. This loneliness was not satisfied by his lovely surroundings.

This inner need for a relationship with a

woman was not met by the sight of the great, towering trees nor the taste of delicious fruits, nuts, and vegetables. Not even such physical activities as strolling among the beautiful orchids and lilies or swimming in the Euphrates River could satisfy Adam's God-given desire for someone to share his life.

The Bible says that God let Adam experience an unfulfilling substitute:

> The Lord God said, "It is not good for the man to be alone. I will make a helper suitable for him."
> Now the Lord God had formed out of the ground all the beasts of the field and all the birds of the air. He brought them to the man to see what he would name them; and whatever the man called each living creature, that was its name (Gen. 2:18-19).

The Lord knew it was not good for Adam to be alone.

Before He gave this first man a relationship with the woman who would be his wife, God let Adam see if maybe a job would fulfill his emptiness.

God assigned the lonely Adam the task of cataloging the Garden's animals. To facilitate this procedure, the Lord caused all the beasts to parade before Adam, who assumed the position of resident zoologist.

Adam spent who knows how many days or weeks or maybe even months giving "names to all the cattle, and to the fowl of the air, and to every beast of the field." When this monumental task was completed, Adam probably felt a great sense of accomplishment, but he was still not happy. In fact, he may have felt worse because the Scriptures tell us "But for Adam no suitable helper was found" (Gen. 2:20).

Do you suppose that as the animals passed before Adam, he had hoped to develop a meaningful relationship with one of them? Although he encountered many intelligent and beautiful creatures — like horses, lions, ostriches, kangaroos, penguins, and even monkeys — none met the need of his heart.

Adam may have even slumped into depression. After all, his task had demonstrated to him that, without a doubt, he was on his own. No other creature could communicate with him on his level.

All the male swans had female swans. Furthermore, they were hatching little swans, which seemed to give them enormous fulfillment.

All the male elephants had female elephants. The male alligators had female alligators, all the male sparrows had female sparrows, and even the male fruit flies had female fruit flies.

And everybody was happy.

Except Adam.

So, he talked to God about it. He asked why he, alone among all the inhabitants of the beautiful Garden, was a loner.

Was Adam really alone? After all, he walked

in the Garden with God every evening. No doubt, there were angels who made continual visitation to the Garden as well.

The Lord must have smiled to himself at Adam's request. After all, He had put that longing, that need for female companionship inside Adam — and into every man who would come after him.

The Lord God knew that this single unit of humanity was not in total fulfillment, so He said aloud, "It is not good for the man to be alone."

And God gave Adam a wife. Eve.

A Dysfunctional Family?

It is most remarkable that God did not begin His creative work in Eve by fashioning a unique person from the dust, as He had with Adam. Instead, the Lord performed the first operation on a human body. The Bible says He took a rib from Adam's side. From this single bone He created the most beautiful creature Adam had ever seen.

The Bible indicates Adam was very glad to see her, as evidenced by his moving words in Genesis 2:23.

The Scriptures do not go into great detail, but apparently she was delighted by him as well. It must have been love at first sight.

Adam, who had been roaming the Garden alone for so long, feeling sorry for himself, now had a beautiful wife.

Their relationship bloomed as they explored the beauty of God's creation together without having to worry about housing, food, or the elements.

Life was exciting, enjoyable, and stress free.

That is, until pride and selfishness entered their hearts.

After eating fruit from the tree of knowledge of good and evil, Adam implicated his wife. "The man said, 'The woman you put here with me — she gave me some fruit from the tree, and I ate it' " (Gen. 3:12).

This must have grieved God, for theirs could have been the perfect marriage.

After the banishment from Eden, Adam and Eve had children.

The Bible records that Eve was apparently amazed when the first boy arrived. "With the help of the Lord I have brought forth a man," she declared at the birth of their firstborn (Gen. 4:1).

Eventually, of course, Cain killed his brother Abel, and this caused much grief for the parents.

But Adam and Eve still had each other.

Today Adam and Eve's relationship might qualify as dysfunctional if analyzed by popular tabloid psychologists. Ann Landers would undoubtedly advise them they would be happier divorced since they had a history of betrayal. Dear Abby would probably tell them that sticking together for the sake of their third newborn son, Seth, really would not be fair to anyone.

A government welfare counselor would note that Adam was a semi-skilled, displaced worker with no income, fired from his last position, devoid of ambition — willing to settle for supporting his family by living off of the land.

And Eve? Obviously, she was co-dependent, according to today's pop psychologists. Why? She wanted to be a *homemaker* and devote her life sacrificially to nurturing dependent children!

The pop psychologist would note with alarm that Adam claimed to have been close friends with God — making him a potential David Koresh or Charles Manson.

The same counselor would be pleased that Eve had been honest enough to confess that while standing around naked beside a sacred tree, she had once had a lengthy philosophical conversation with a snake. It had told her how to be as wise as God — making Eve a potential success on the New Age speaker's circuit.

Fortunately, there were no humanistic advisors around to further damage Adam and Eve's rocky marriage.

The Mystery of Marriage

Although their relationship was marred by heartache and disappointment, the unity between Adam and Eve was never broken. As far as they — and God — were concerned, they were "one flesh."

This unique relationship is what I call "the mystery of marriage."

In His mystery of marriage, God decided each of us should have a rich relationship with another person. He ordained that we should have a fulfilling companionship with one other person.

The mystery of marriage is that two persons, with two separate minds, two separate willpowers, two separate sets of emotions, can come together and break down their own willpower and their own desires in favor of the other one.

The two become one. They enjoy pleasing one another. That doesn't work with an animal. It doesn't work in any other creature except mankind. Two people unite as one person. As long as they flow in that unity, it is the happiest situation that a person can have on planet Earth. There is no greater joy than the happiness of a home where the two have become one.

God has given mankind a wondrous gift in marriage. A solid marriage lays the foundation for a secure home. That's why this unique relationship must be constructed carefully according to His blueprint.

Let's look at the building blocks that form the framework of a unified marriage relationship.

2

C h a p t e r

Framework for a Solid Marriage

Therefore what God has joined together, let man not separate.
— Mark 10:9

Society today says it is okay just to live together and that you can have a home without marriage. Is it true?

No. You can live in a house, but that doesn't make a home. A home has to have a married couple there — a man and a woman who love each other and who produce children to build a nation. People who promiscuously have sex with one another are not a marriage nor a family.

Couples who live together don't want to be confined to commitment or loyalty, so they say, "Well, I'll just have sex with you awhile." They can break up anytime. There's no law to bind them or keep them together. Either of them can walk out whenever they wish because they have made no commitment one to another. They lack a covenant with God that vows "I'll live with you until death do us part."

As a result, they are always suspicious of each other. When they walk out of the house in the morning, they never know if their "significant other" will be there when they return or not. Their relationship lacks the framework on which a marriage is built — commitment and trust.

Yet the world keeps trying to tell us that such a "lifestyle" is the same as a home. What absolute foolishness.

Ours is an era when vows are easily broken and commitments are casually discarded. How can we stem the tide? How can we build and maintain a united marriage?

Let's get out the blueprint and see how God would have us structure our relationship.

A Commitment for Life

The mystery of marriage relies heavily on mutual commitment — one to another. The husband and wife must be totally committed to each other, physically, emotionally, and certainly in their spirits. With this framework, they can stand united to resist the evil forces working to divide them.

What do I mean by commitment?

Look at Ephesians 5. It is a favorite of most Christian men because it tells women to submit themselves to their husbands. Most men like sermons on that subject and delight in poking their wives' noses in that verse and demanding complete obedience.

Such men, however, don't read far enough. Verse 25 says that husbands are to love their wives "just as Christ loved the church and gave himself up for her."

Think about that.

If a husband loves his wife with the same kind of love that Jesus has for the Church, he must be willing to sacrifice his own selfish desires.

What kind of love did Christ have for His church?

He died for us. He gave His body for His church! He was nailed upon a crude cross because of His unselfish love for you!

Now, how are you, as a husband, supposed to love your wife? Is it to be a demanding love, requiring that your wife submit to your every whim? Was that how Jesus loved the Church?

No.

Sacrificial love is not a selfish love. It is a giving love. That's the type of love God calls upon husbands to have for their wives.

I realize that sacrificial love is not a popular notion. Most people — particularly men — dislike self-denial. We prefer instant gratification.

If someone wants a pizza, they call out and

the delivery person has to rush it to their doorstep within 30 minutes or it is free. If someone wants a diamond ring, they tune into the cable TV shopping club and charge one on their spouse's credit card so it can be sent overnight express.

No, we do not live in a cultural environment that nurtures the concept of sacrificial love. Yet, that is the kind of commitment the Lord requires of Christian husbands.

We live in a time when married couples split up for no better reason than one of them just doesn't feel "love" anymore.

Society tells us that love is a feeling. That's true, but love is more than a warm fuzzy feeling; it is commitment to another human being that involves giving up something of ourselves.

Marriage requires commitment. The nuptial covenant is only as good as the commitment that backs it up. In today's society, there is a widespread hesitancy to become committed to anything, particularly to another person.

---

*Marriage is not a temporary
arrangement. It is a
commitment for life.*

A successful marriage must be exclusive, involving no other people except the husband and the wife. The relationship between a husband and wife is intended to be exclusive — one man with one woman in one relationship. This relationship affects the man's relationship with all other women, and the woman's relationship with all other men.

Each spouse commits to "forsake all others." That means, if a man's wife and his mother are drowning, he is supposed to rescue his wife first, then go back and get his mother.

It means that if a good-looking hunk of a man struts into the wife's life and waves a million dollars under her nose to have an illicit affair with him, she doesn't even have to think about it. She is committed to her one and only.

With a lifetime commitment of "I'm with you in this no matter what," there is a deep sense of security.

The closest thing to the marriage commitment is the relationship between a Christian and Jesus.

Every true Christian says to the world, "I have a peculiar relationship with one person, Jesus Christ, that affects my relationship with everybody else. I am faithful to Him first."

Our relationship with Jesus must go beyond our initial salvation experience where we go forward at a crusade or pray with a television evangelist. We must continually acknowledge our commitment to loving and serving the Lord with our whole heart.

Our marriage commitment works the same way and must be more than the once-only vows of the wedding ceremony. A marriage needs continual reaffirmation of that commitment. We need to speak it with our lips, telling our partner that we are theirs — and theirs alone.

Marriage is not a temporary arrangement. It is a commitment for life. That is why wise men long ago built into the words of the marriage service: "For better, for worse, for richer, for poorer, in sickness and in health, till death us do part."

Resolving Conflicts

No human being is perfect; we all know that.

In marriage, however, it is essential to choose to believe the best about our mates in all situations. On the surface that may sound easy, but what if your mother accuses your spouse of something?

Your marriage commitment obligates you to take the side of your spouse. But how can you turn your back on your mother?

Read Matthew 19:5-6. It is bluntly clear! A man shall leave his mother and father and shall become one flesh with his wife. Furthermore, "Therefore what God has joined together, let man not separate." That means you are obligated to be loyal to your spouse.

Did you know that in most American courts of law, a spouse cannot be forced to testify against a marital partner? That's because, under the Fifth Amendment, you don't have to testify against yourself. Apparently, United States law recognizes that a husband and wife are one.

In daily, practical matters, this commitment means that you always give your mate the benefit of the doubt. Always assume that your spouse did not intend to hurt you — even if shouted words were harsh or unkind. Even if your mate's actions may not seem to be good, believe that their intent was for a good reason.

He or she may be immature in some ways and may act out of jealousy or revenge, but you must be merciful and slow to get angry. Instead of reacting to your spouse's accusing words against you, ask yourself if his or her words are cries for help. By avoiding accusation against the one you love, you will find yourself with fewer grounds for conflict, fewer silent grudges, and fewer hurt feelings.

Over the years of our marriage, I learned never to go to sleep with an anger unspoken. This doesn't mean that as my head hit my pillow, I lashed out against my wife — accusing her for something that had angered me.

No, it means that I did not go to sleep until I had talked to her and told her that I was angry about something she said or did. I explained my hurt and how she had wounded me. I didn't make her guess or force her to suffer in silence until she could figure out why I was pouting. Although I may have had to swallow my pride, I found it best to get my grievances out in the open.

I hate to tell you the times when, by talking out such disagreements, I turned out to be the one who was less than perfect. In pointing out her mistakes, it was often revealed that I had done something to precipitate her negative reaction to me. My wife would point out — and I would realize — that I had been the one at fault.

Fortunately, Louise was always kind and gentle when mentioning my mistakes. I was able to take criticism from her because I knew how much she loved me and because I assumed she was not trying to hurt me. We had a mutual trust that allowed us to say virtually anything to one another without fear.

Trust is assuming in every situation the very best of your spouse. It is believing that your mate's intentions are pure. Trust is the opposite of suspicion.

Let me give you an example. We know that we must never think evil of God, according to James 1:13. He is the Almighty. What He does is always right, always just, and always good.

It is the same way in marriage.

Always assume the best of your spouse. Don't accuse.

When a regiment goes to war, the unit that stays closest together is the one willing to make the ultimate sacrifice — one soldier giving his life for his buddies. They are willing to die for each other.

During a conflict, one soldier may ask another: "Cover me while I go to the next hill over there."

The other young soldier grabs his machine gun and whirls it in every direction, looking for an enemy — covering his friend.

When a man and a woman are married, they become covered. They are covered with each other's mind — the two minds become one. They are covered with each other's emotions — the emotions change and become one great feeling flowing through their lives. In drawing themselves together through integrity, their relationship is built on that wonderful knowing called "trust."

Building with Trust

How important is trust in such marriages? How is it earned? How is it developed?

Trust is developed through experience. You can't have trust without experience. You don't know whether the limb of a tree will hold you up until you climb out and sit on it. Then you know very soon whether the limb has enough strength to support you.

Trust is going from limb to limb — discovering what can hold your weight.

A happy marriage is built upon trust. Trust is built upon experience, and experience creates knowledge. You can say, "I know how she (or he) will react in this situation because we've been through this before."

A man and woman should be more deeply in love after the first year of marriage than they were on the first night of their honeymoon. Maybe that's why, according to the Old Testament, recently married Israelite soldiers were given 12 months of leave from their duties.

"If a man has recently married, he must not be sent to war or have any other duty laid on him. For one year he is to be free to stay at home and bring happiness to the wife he has married" (Deut. 24:5).

Without any external distractions, the couple could get to know one another by experience, and that experience would create trust to last for a lifetime. They became bound together until all of hell could not shake them loose. From that time on, the thought never crossed their minds that they would ever be separated one from another.

Trust grows stronger and stronger as husbands and wives have more and more experience with each other. Their faith in their spouse's character strengthens, knowing that he or she will do what is right and not betray the trust of the other.

You know that you know. You're sure that you're sure. Trust is born within us through day by day experience.

In all our years of marriage, I never once looked around to see to whom my wife was talking. I trusted Louise so much that I knew, whatever she was saying, it was appropriate. I knew from experience that she never spoke anything that was not good — about me or the family or anyone.

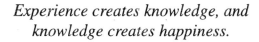

Experience creates knowledge, and knowledge creates happiness.

Proverbs 31:11 describes the godly wife and says, "Her husband has full confidence in her."

If a husband comes home night after night to find that his wife is somewhere else, his trust in her may be called into question.

Whenever she comes running in late, half out of breath, he is likely to ask her, "Where have you been?"

"Oh, just around," she may respond evasively.

"I'm your husband, I have a right to know where you have been," he demands.

If she answers, "Oh, visiting some of my friends," doubts are raised in his mind.

She may think she's asserting her independence when, in reality, she is undermining the marriage relationship. As a result, her husband's trust begins to die.

Why? Because he caught her in bed with the mailman? No. Because she won't level with him! She has kept something from him and won't share everything with him. As a result, the framework of their marriage is weakened and may eventually collapse.

How do you build trust in a marriage? You build it with your actions. Through consistent behavior in different circumstances, you show your mate that you can be trusted. Then he or she will know how you will react in difficult situations.

Once he or she knows you can be trusted, your mate will respond with more openness and trustworthiness on his or her part. As a result, you will develop a sense of pure confidence in one another.

That kind of trust constructs a secure framework that can withstand the onslaught of many storms in your marriage.

The Two-by-Fours of Trust

The strength of the framework of trust in a marriage depends on the width and depth of the planks that form the structure. That strength comes from seeking the truth diligently.

Integrity in your relationship must be more important than anything else. That means always telling the truth and being honest in all things. It means truthfulness and honesty in your actions.

With those building blocks in place, trust will result. Your spouse will have confidence in you, and your children will know they can rely on you.

In a trusting relationship, a husband can leave home and know his wife will act the same while he is away as she does when he is present. The wife, when her husband has to go away on business, will be secure and confident that he can be trusted to behave with integrity and faithfulness.

Without integrity, a husband worries constantly that his wife is stepping out on him or emptying the bank account or letting the children run wild.

Without integrity, the wife lives in fear that her husband is chasing skirts and lusting after every young woman who crosses his path. She begins to suspect that he is hiding money from her and trembles in fear that he is going to leave her high and dry.

Unwilling to accept God's totally dependable absolutes, the dishonest husband and wife themselves become undependable. They do whatever they wish, and as a result can no longer trust themselves or each other. It is not possible for them to build a happy home because they are unstable and double-minded.

When cracks develop in the framework of trust, jealousy can creep in and invade the home. As a result, anger, bitterness, and accusations rush in like termites to rob the marriage of its love, joy, and contentment — and eventually destroy the relationship between husband and wife.

A lack of integrity, honesty, and truth lead many couples into divorce court where the marriage dissolves into a heap of rubble because they can no longer trust each other.

Is There a Plan "B"?

How can we have honesty and integrity in our home, in our families, and in our marriages?

First of all, we have to agree on what we are talking about. What is honesty? What is integrity?

They both mean truth. And what is truth today — in a moral climate in which everything is relative and there are no absolutes?

God is truth. He is unchanging.

How did Jesus advise the rich young ruler who came to Him seeking truth? (See Matt. 19:16-21.)

The young man asked Jesus, "Teacher, what good thing must I do to get eternal life?"

Jesus answered that he must keep God's commandments.

The young man persisted, as Jesus knew he would, asking, "Which ones?"

Jesus replied, "Do not murder, do not commit adultery, do not steal, do not give false testimony, honor your father and mother, and love your neighbor as yourself."

"All these I have kept," the young man said. "What do I still lack?"

Jesus answered, "If you want to be perfect, go, sell your possessions and give to the poor. . . . Then come, follow me."

The young man's search for the truth ended there. He was not that interested.

If finding truth meant sacrificing everything he owned, then the young man decided he would settle for second best.

That's the way it is with society today. Many people are settling for second best in their lives and their marriages.

What did the young man really want from the Lord? His question was not so much about rules to be followed, but about the "meaning of life." This search is ultimately an appeal for absolutes. When the world finds them, however, it blinks in consternation and continues looking elsewhere.

The Bible says that the rich young man turned away. He could not sacrifice his possessions. *They* possessed him. His worldly goods meant more to him than eternal life!

I see people make that choice everyday. Their possessions, their career, their lusts, their pleasures are more important than ensuring they will not burn in hell forever.

They squint uncomfortably when you show them the truth, and they ask if there is a "Plan B." They want something else that won't require them to give up the things they love.

The Absolute Truth

Only in Jesus Christ can you and I find what is absolute.

Only God can answer the questions about what is true, because He alone made the world. He established the laws of nature that keep the moon in the sky, the earth in its orbit, and the stars in place.

He invented gravity — an absolute that cannot be denied. He invented time, another absolute that cannot be subverted. He made the absolute rules governing mathematics and physics.

He invented the divinely ordained guidelines, too, by which mankind is supposed to live.

Mankind can accept the absolutes of nature, but many people have trouble when it comes to following God's rules for living. They say His commands are "narrow-minded, old fashioned, too restricting." To avoid the truth, they listen to Satan's lies that there is another way.

To ask about truth ultimately means to turn toward God. He alone is worthy of being loved with all our heart and with all our soul and with all our mind, according to Matthew 22:37.

God is the only source of man's happiness. "I am the Lord your God, who brought you out of Egypt, out of the land of slavery," proclaims Exodus 20:2-3.

God remains the only constant and true model for morality. "Be holy because I, the Lord your God, am holy," promises Leviticus 19:2. "I will walk among you and be your God, and you will be my people," assures Leviticus 26:12.

"Hear, O Israel: The Lord our God, the Lord is one," proclaims Deuteronomy 6:4-7, "Love the Lord your God with all your heart and with all your soul and with all your strength. These commandments that I give you today are to be upon your hearts. Impress them on your children. Talk about them when you sit at home and when you walk along the road, when you lie down and when you get up."

Truth is found by walking humbly with Him in doing justice and in loving kindness, says Micah 6:8.

"Holy, holy, holy is the Lord Almighty," proclaims Isaiah 6:3.

Mankind, however, doesn't want to do it God's way. Most people are willing to settle for second best and prefer Satan's deceptions. The devil's lies allow them to tiptoe around the truth and figure out human compromises and easy alternatives.

That's what happened with the rich young ruler.

Jesus sadly watched him walk away after he refused to give up his possessions. Then the Lord turned to His disciples and told them, ". . . everyone who has left houses or brothers or sisters or father or mother or children or fields, for my sake will receive a hundred times as much and will inherit eternal life" (Matt. 19:29).

If only the rich young ruler had stuck around to hear the bottom line! If he was really interested in the profitability of following Jesus, then, he should have heard that if he sacrificed all that he had for Jesus's sake, he would have ended up with a vast return on his money! One hundredfold!

That's 100 times more than what he had in the beginning! If he had sacrificed three barns full of grain and 20 camels, he would have ended up with 300 barns and 2,000 camels! Plus eternal life!

All the talk about sacrifice, however, turned the young man off, so he wandered away in search of second best. Truth suddenly wasn't so important after all. It would cost too much.

Foolishly, he stomped off before Jesus got to the punch line.

That young man represents the world today. Most people reject Christ before they ever read the Bible. They close their eyes to the truth when it gets in the way of their second-best solutions.

The Source of All Truth

Anyone who wishes to understand himself thoroughly — not just partially or superficially — must — amid their unrest, uncertainty, and even their weakness and sinfulness — seek the truth in Christ.

Jesus is the Alpha and the Omega of human history, according to Revelation 1:8.

To those who are honest with God, the Holy Spirit will open the Scriptures and reveal the Father's will, teaching us the truth.

Jesus, as a patient and sensitive teacher, answered the rich young man by taking him, as it were, by the hand and leading him step by step to the truth.

"There is only One who is good," Jesus said in Matthew 19:17 "If you want to enter life, obey the commandments."

In Mark 10:18 this incident is retold and the question is phrased this way: "Why do you call me good? . . . No one is good — except God alone."

Before answering the question, Jesus wished the young man to have a clear idea of why He had asked His question. Jesus pointed out to him — and to all of us — that the truth to the question, "What good must I do to have eternal life?" can only be found by turning our minds and hearts over to the One who is good.

"Oops!" they say. "That asks too much!"

They reserve the right to do whatever they want. And so, they waltz right past the truth and go on to wherever they can find answers that tickle their ears and make them feel good in their sin.

Satan is always waiting with counterfeits. He soothes their ruffled feathers, assuring them that there are many truths. He comforts them, telling them that they can be as wise as God and come up with their own answers.

"Sure," Satan whispers, "you can do whatever you want. Sure, whatever is right for you. Yes, yes, there are many different roads to truth."

Sorry, it doesn't work that way.

Jesus alone is the Way, the Truth and the Life, according to my Bible — and yours. We cannot come unto the Father except by Him.

Jesus is the door. When we knock, it opens. But we cannot burst through the wall or climb through the window. We cannot drop through the chimney. We can come in only through Him.

That's what makes Christianity different from

Islam or Buddhism or Hinduism. If you are foolish enough to dig into those pagan theologies, you will find that they have a lot in common with Christianity. They have so much in common that many non-Christians proclaim that eventually there will be one world religion in which the good from all faiths will be combined and respected.

Actually, it is already here. It is the New Age movement, an assortment of mysticism and hocus-pocus from Native American superstitions, ancient mystery cults, astrology, spiritualism, witchcraft, and the "old religions" of Europe and Asia. This New Age religion proclaims that a new, sophisticated way has been found for each of us to become little gods, attaining our own enlightenment and salvation.

That is a lie.

Our salvation is possible only through Jesus Christ. And that truth puts our Christian faith in opposition to all the others.

The bottom line is that all other religions are counterfeits designed by Satan to seduce mankind into false peace, false hope, and false security.

Jesus is the only Way.

Any sincere search for truth finds One Source of absolute truth — our Almighty God, our Creator, the Source of *all that is*.

3

C h a p t e r

Cementing Your Relationship

Place me like a seal over your heart,
like a seal on your arm; for love is
as strong as death. . . .
— Song of Sol. 8:6

A man about 45 years old walked into my office in South Bend a few years ago. He was crying.

I said, "What's wrong?"

"My wife's run off," he moaned. "We've been married 25 years, and she's left me."

I said, "Tell me what happened."

"We own our home here in South Bend and also a nice house up by the lake in Michigan. A few months ago a guy selling vacuum cleaners came by and showed my wife how his sweeper could pick up dirt off the carpet. She decided to buy a sweeper from him. Before he left he asked, 'Could you give me a cup of coffee?' So they had coffee together.

"The next day he came back and said, 'I just stopped to see how the new sweeper is working. It might need a little oil or something.' And before he left he hugged her.

"The next day he was back again and said, 'I just wondered if your husband appreciates you. You're so beautiful. Has he told you lately how pretty you are?'

"She told him, 'Well, no, he hasn't.'

"He said, 'Well, you're just about the sweetest person I've ever met. Has he ever told you how nice you are?'

" 'No.'

"Before he left this time he just laid her down on the bed and committed adultery with her. That began to happen almost every day. Finally, she just left me a note and said, 'I'm leaving.' "

The man was brokenhearted.

I said, "It may be too late, but there is something you can learn from this. Your wife was not satisfied with two houses and two cars. She wanted you."

"What do you mean?" he asked.

"What did you do in the evenings?"

"Well," he said, "I worked in the basement, making this and that. But it was always for her."

"She didn't believe it," I told him. "Actually,

I don't believe it either. It was for your own satisfaction."

No woman nor any man can be happy with *things.* Very rich people get divorces — money does not hold them together. We've got to have something more basic than riches or wealth or homes to be happy. Life gets downright bleak for the lonesome woman married to a man who won't talk to her.

I gave this distraught husband some suggestions on how to win back his wife, but I never heard from him again. I don't think they got back together.

During my years in the ministry, I have counseled dozens of couples whose marriages were in trouble because they had never learned how to communicate with one another.

Communication is the mortar that holds a marriage together. If you talk together, you stay together.

To allow ourselves to be open with our partners, we need to trust them. To trust them, we need to know them. To know them, they need to trust us and open up to us.

Opening up to each other is a risky business. There is always the possibility that you might get your feelings hurt.

That's why some husbands are not communicative. Most are bound by the image that the world expects them to be strong and silent like John Wayne in the cowboy movies or like Teddy Roosevelt who spoke softly but carried a big stick. Men think they are supposed to be tough guys who keep their emotions under control.

Women, however, thrive on expressions of emotion. A wife needs to hear those special words: "I love you." It does something to a woman that a man just can't understand.

A husband, on the other hand, can go years without hearing that his wife loves him. He figures if she's still fixing his favorite meals and ironing his shirts and caring for his children that she loves him. Men don't need to have regular verbal expressions the way women do. That's why it's so difficult for some husbands to understand why their wives are so sentimental about birthdays and anniversaries.

Wives need to hear their husbands say — out loud in an audible voice on a daily basis — "I love you."

Becoming Best Friends

I learned early in my marriage that my wife and I benefitted greatly from sharing our thoughts and concerns and worries and joys. This required some discipline on my part, however, since I was not a natural listener. It took a while, but I realized that she was much more content when I would shut up and listen to what she needed to say.

If I would be at my desk writing a book, my wife would often come in and want to tell me something. Instead of brushing her off, I knew it was time to put my work aside and talk to her. She needed my undivided attention. I knew if she didn't get it from me she'd either be miserable or find someone else who would listen to her.

My wife enjoyed expressing herself to me. God made her that way, so I decided I had better just appreciate it. After a while, I learned to love hearing Louise express her feelings because it gave me a glimpse into her heart.

My wife was my very best friend.

How can you be friends with your spouse?

It is mostly a matter of your will. Resolve that the two of you will be "best friends" from now on.

Friendship is based on emotional attachment, but that is not enough. It is also based on familiarity. One reason that a friend is a friend is that you are used to being around that person. You know what to expect from him or her.

If you want to be a friend to your spouse, then you need to spend time together.

Many young couples fail to realize that marriage is not just a "period of adjustment" it is a *lifetime* of learning to adjust to one another. Many marriages fail because of an unwillingness on the part of one or both partners to re-adjust their habits, their thinking, and/or their approach to life

A young man may run around with a bunch of boys his own age up until the day of his wedding. But the moment he's married, he doesn't do that anymore. He's a married man now with the responsibility of a wife, and he must adjust his life accordingly. If he doesn't, he will fail to develop a lasting friendship with his wife.

The wife has to make adjustments, too. She may be used to talking for hours on the phone with friends or spending time shopping with her mother. If she tries to carry those habits over into her marriage, her new husband will feel neglected and unimportant. As a married woman, she must learn to share her deepest secrets with her husband and spend her spare time with him.

When a husband and wife marry, the two become one and should go places together, do things together, and learn to communicate with one another.

Learning to Listen

Making simple, little adjustments early in marriage can prevent complicated, expensive problems later. Still, it's never to late to learn to adjust your lifestyle to one that pleases your spouse — and saves your marriage.

Where do you start? By listening to your mate. Learn what he or she thinks is important in the daily routines of life and how you can adjust your habits to ones that please your spouse.

If you go into the bathroom and leave it looking as if a storm has just passed through, you're going to have to adjust to cleaning it up before you leave.

If she says, "Toothpaste is expensive these days. Why do you leave the top off and have it squirting out onto the counter?" Then you need to say, "You're right, honey. I'll try to remember to screw on the lid."

Learn to respect the wishes of your spouse no matter how trivial or seemingly unnecessary. If is it important to him or her, it should at least warrant your attention and cooperation.

The way you communicate may also need some fine tuning. If you're used to blowing your top at the least offense, you are going to have to adjust. Why? Out of respect for the one you love. You can't start screaming at your spouse the way you yelled at your brothers and sisters before you were married. If you do, you're going to break the fabric that binds a husband and wife together.

Marriage is a new world, a new life. It's the blending of two people who were brought up in two different homes and used to different ways. Both have to adjust if they are committed to keeping their marriage together.

I have seen many marriages dissolve because one or both mates wanted to act as if they were still single. They weren't adjusting to marriage or to their spouse. As a result, when a misunderstanding arose, they had no common ground on which to stand, and the result was divorce.

Adjustment is not just required of newlyweds. It is ongoing. To make marriage work you have to be flexible and considerate of each other.

This great unwritten beatitude needs to be posted on every refrigerator door in America: "Blessed are the flexible."

We cannot expect to live in harmony with our mate and remain stuck in our ways. To do so is to be selfish, self-centered, and unloving.

Understanding your mate's likes and dislikes develops over time, but it begins with a desire to please your husband or wife in the daily routine of life. That only comes about by spending time with one another.

I don't mean watching a TV show together. When you do that, you may be sitting together and holding hands, but your attention is focused on the idiot box. Instead of enjoying quality time together, you are spending time with your TV, listening to it, investing your emotions and your interest in whatever it has for you. You are not involved with each other.

So turn the TV off and talk to your spouse. Make a mutual commitment that you will spend time together daily. Arrange your schedule so that you can sit down and talk.

What about? It doesn't matter.

Ask, "What did you do today?"

Most men find the details of life to be trivial, but women thrive on details so don't just indulge her a little. Be willing to listen to her complaints about the children or recounts of the money she saved on coupons at the grocery store. If she works outside the home, learn something about her job and the people she works with.

At the same time, you, too, must be willing to share the daily trivialities of your life. Tell your wife what you had for lunch, how you solved a problem at work, what the boss said, what bugs you about your job, etc.

Before long, you'll both have a deeper appreciation of what the other faces on a day to day basis. Then you will know how to pray for one another, how to encourage the other on the bad days, and how to advise your spouse in difficult situations.

After all, isn't that what marriage is all about? Living life together and being there for one another in the daily grind?

How to Carry on a Conversation

Conversation is an art that few people ever master, but it actually requires little more than self-less interest in the other person and the willingness to share something of yourself. If you and your spouse are having trouble communicating, here are some practical suggestions on how to get started.

Talk to your spouse about whatever is interesting to you. Both of you are interested in the children and their activities, so this provides an immediate common source of conversation.

Talk about things going on at church. Are you planning to help out with the missionary dinner? Has John down the street been asked to serve on the Stewardship Committee?

Talk about the PTA, the FBI, or UFOs. It doesn't matter. What *is* important is that you talk to each other.

I love keeping up with the news, but my wife would only watch a news program if the subject interested her. In fact, she rarely watched all of "60 Minutes" or any of the network news shows. She did, however, like hearing my version of the news.

In fact, she prefered me to Dan Rather or Tom Brokaw or Peter Jennings. She wouldn't listen to them, but she paid avid attention when I told her about the latest trouble in Israel or new attempts to help the people of Bosnia. I liked knowing that she respected my opinions about world events.

One important way to stimulate communication is to ask your spouse for advice. Seek out his or her opinion.

Of course, conversation cannot be a one-sided affair. It is not a conversation if you chatter away incessantly at your spouse. Nor is it a conversation if you do an imitation of a cigar-store Indian, sitting silently without expression or comment.

Learn to listen carefully to what your spouse says. Then react to it with a comment of some kind.

If your mate says something absolutely puzzling to you — something on a subject that you know absolutely nothing about — turn their comment into a question.

Suppose the husband says, "You know, I never have understood why such a great player as Nolan Ryan would get so mad about being beaned as he did that time that he jumped Robin Ventura. I expect that sort of thing in ice hockey, but not baseball."

Now, what do you say?

Odds are you do not remember the time that Ryan came to blows with Ventura on national television. You may have no idea whether Ryan was a baseball player or a sumo wrestler.

So, how do you keep the conversation going?

Hang onto the last thing that he said. Turn it into a question. Say to him "Why didn't you expect that?"

He will probably answer something like: "Because baseball is baseball. We're talking about America's national pastime for goodness sake. Can you imagine Babe Ruth charging a pitcher? Can you see Lou Gehrig or Shoeless Joe Jackson duking it out with Ty Cobb? No way."

Now it is your turn again. Try to turn the conversation to something more on your wavelength, such as, "Did your dad play catch with you when you were a little boy?"

Most dads play a little catch with their sons at some point in their lives. It's during those times that fathers and sons talk about life and girls and growing up.

The hit baseball movie *Field of Dreams* was basically about a man who could not deal with life until he had one more chance to play catch with his dad. The Robert Redford film *The Natural* ends happily when the tortured hero finally finds peace by playing catch with his long-lost son.

In our society today, many grown men who did not play catch with their dad feel deprived and cheated. Your husband will more than likely have a lot to say about his dad and playing catch.

You can steer the conversation easily from there. Ask about his relationship with his dad. Ask him what kind of dad he wants to be. Before you know it, you will realize you can master the art of meaningful conversation with your mate.

Sharing Feelings

Husbands, suppose your wife tells you, "You

ought to see how Lisa did her breakfast nook. Her old, quaint cabinets now have a pie-safe look that matches her antique, aluminum backsplash. She re-upholstered the settee with a mix of plaids, chintzes, and toiles giving it all a, you know, sort of informal, country ambiance."

The average man would grunt and turn the page of his newspaper. You, however, have made a commitment to communicate. So, what are you going to say? How about, "Sort of informal and country, you say? What does it remind you of?"

Now, pay attention to her answer. She will probably say something about the breakfast room reminding her of somebody else's — maybe her mom's, her best friend's in the second grade, her grandmother's, her next door neighbor's back in the old neighborhood — or whatever.

Listen carefully and move the conversation in the direction of something that interests you. For example, she might say, "I like it because it reminds me of my Aunt Suzie. She was married to Uncle Frank who taught me everything I know about professional football."

Football? Now you are talking!

But what if you hate football? *That happens.* The wife is an avid sports fan and the husband would rather be rewiring antique radios.

Well, do the same thing you did before — keep listening for her to mention something that does interest you. Or maybe this is the time that you bare your soul to her and admit your deepest, darkest secret — that you have always hated football.

After all, she is your wife. She will find out anyway. Tell her about the world's most ignorant coach who in the fourth grade made fun of the way you ran — and killed your love of sports forever. Tell her how you felt.

Very few men — or women for that matter — are willing or even able to reveal their innermost feelings. It is hard to reveal their hopes and dreams with even their closest friend — at least at first. It is the rare person who can talk about their hurts and doubts and fears before they sincerely trust the listener. Most people are afraid of being told, "You shouldn't feel that way," or "That's crazy."

Just as Romans 8:35-39 promises us that nothing can separate us from the love of Christ, so nothing should be allowed to come between you and your mate that keeps you from communicating.

Silence does not make a happy marriage. So, talk. Talk when you are happy. Talk when you are sad. Talk when you are angry instead of giving your mate the silent treatment. Don't pout to get your way. Talk!

Communicate your feelings, thoughts, problems, and failures. Share your joys as well as your fears. Both the positives and the negatives in our lives need expression. Talk them out with the one you love. As you do, you will find the bond between you growing stronger, cementing your relationship in a firm unity of mutual respect.

Keeping the Slate Clean

Communication in a marriage involves more

than learning how to carry on a meaninful conversation and share feelings. Learning to communicate
is also the essential to resolving conflicts and keeping your relationship on a steady course.

Whenever you get two human beings together
for any length of time, conflicts are bound to arise.
This is a fact of life, but we need not see it as an
insurmountable problem. Let's face it: We all make
mistakes. We all offend others with our actions and
our words — no matter how well-meaning we try to
be.

The difficulty arises when we have to face
the person we have offended. Why? Because the
hardest act for any human is to admit being wrong
and to ask for forgiveness.

It's a good idea to clean the slate before you
go to bed at night. Turn to your spouse and say, "Dar-
ling, have I hurt you any today?"

Be prepared to hear what a jerk you have
been.

Don't get angry. Be sorry and repentant. Ask
for forgiveness. Just say, "Would you forgive me?
I'm sorry. I certainly didn't mean to hurt you, it just
happened that way. Forgive me."

No doubt your mate will say, "Yes, you are
forgiven." Then you hug and kiss and you can sleep
soundly knowing the slate is clean.

Don't wait until you or your spouse are half-
asleep or getting groggy. There's nothing more irri-
tating than pouring out your heart to a spouse who
begins snoring. If you have been guilty of dozing
off in mid-discussion, then remain sitting up until

your husband or wife is finished talking.

My wife and I would never go to sleep if we had an unresolved problem between us. Actually, I do not believe that we ever had a major argument. We did, of course, have separate opinions on some issues, but these were minor areas that did not affect our relationship.

If you are the one who has been offended or hurt, keep your focus on the issue at hand. Nobody likes to have their faults cited — particularly if we are told that we have to make a list of changes before forgiveness can be "granted." That sort of attitude weakens the very foundation of any marriage.

Keeping mental ledgers, however, is no way to get the process underway. In fact, it is much harder to resolve a conflict when we are presented with a list of wrongs that must be righted.

First Corinthians 13:5 specifically says that love doesn't keep "a record of wrongs." If you go back to the original Greek, the verse basically says that love doesn't bear malice, doesn't keep an accounting of past problems, and isn't resentful.

In the heat of a marital argument is never the time to dredge up past offenses. When sin is confessed and repented, the healing of God's power is received!

If God has cleared your spouse's record, don't you be guilty of refusing to do the same. Remember, it is Satan who keeps lists with which he accuses believers.

We are commanded to forgive.

Take the Initiative

Most agitations in a home begin very small. If they are not handled immediately, however, a molehill can turn into a mountain. Don't hold that problem over for the next day. If both of you will say "I'm sorry," then you can start anew.

If the wound is allowed to fester, however, it can spread to other areas of the relationship until neither of you can even remember how the conflict started.

So, take the initiative. If you sense that your mate is upset, ask what is wrong. Don't get defensive if you are accused unfairly. Just listen.

Sincerely say these simple words: "I'm sorry." Then listen carefully to his or her response.

Have the decency and humility to give your spouse the benefit of the doubt. Even if the accusations are completely off-base, don't fire back. Don't get defensive. And never play the wounded martyr.

If the person you love — who is flesh of your flesh — feels that you were inconsiderate, offensive, or selfish, then you must have done *something*.

Begin with a forgiving spirit on your part, and diffuse the rising emotions before they flare into a major conflict.

Be willing to say, "I'm sorry. I had no idea. I want your forgiveness."

Men, it may be something simple that you have neglected, such as leaving your underwear on the floor or not lifting the toilet seat. It is very easy to get irked when your spouse constantly harps about such mundane things.

However, if she is constantly upset about something, ask yourself if you love her enough to clean up your act. How absurd it would be to sacrifice your marriage over your refusal to put your clean — or dirty — laundry where it belongs.

Habits are hard to break. If you are absent minded and do such infuriating things as forgetting which toothbrush is yours, then ask your spouse to pray with you that the Lord will help you overcome your thoughtlessness.

After all, it is hard to hold a grudge against somebody who has asked for forgiveness, who has prayed for help to change, and obviously is making an effort to remedy the situation.

If you will do that, you can have a happy home.

You cannot live in peace and tranquillity, however, if your household is filled with quarreling, unforgiveness, unrepentance, and constant accusation.

Remember, we all need forgiveness from time to time.

Maintaining a Happy Home

There may come times in your marriage when you genuinely have been wronged in a large way. If your spouse has an affair, your hurt will be enormous.

If your spouse is dishonest with you about finances — and squanders your savings or a family inheritance — forgiving can seem impossible.

What if you or your children are victims of

abuse from your spouse? Forgiveness may seem the most difficult thing you have ever attempted. But for your own sake, you must forgive.

Since you are human, you might think it impossible to forgive someone. That's right — as long as you try it without God. When we come to Christ, our attitudes change and our minds begin to seek the Father. This is in direct contrast to the ways of the world.

Forgiveness might come slowly, but it is the only way to happiness in a bad situation.

"Now that you have purified yourselves by obeying the truth so that you have sincere love for your brothers, love one another deeply, from the heart" (1 Pet. 1:22).

Jesus told us to pray for those who hurt us. The Bible doesn't say anything about holding onto bitterness and letting it poison us. How many diseases could be washed away through the healing medicine of forgiveness!

Jesus said to us, ". . . Love your enemies and pray for those who persecute you . . ." (Matt. 5:44).

If your spouse refuses to repent, you should try in your own heart to still forgive him or her, but you are not required by God to be foolish. If your safety or health or that of your children is at risk, you may have to get away from danger.

Even in the most extreme situation, when an abused spouse flees or if your children must be rescued from a nightmarish situation, do what you must. But forgive. Pray that your spouse will change. Pray fervently that your marriage will be restored.

Forgiveness comes in big and little packages. God has forgiven us. We must learn to be forgiving — like Jesus was. If we seek to be like Him, we can certainly have successful marriages and happy homes.

The marriage relationship goes round and round, the same as a wedding band on the finger of a man and a woman. There is no end to it; it is a circle. Spouses are together forever, throughout life. The covenant that we make is for our whole life, not just a part of it.

A good marriage requires constant work for the relationship to grow and mature. And the seeds of a healthy marriage begin with the little things like remembering to say "I love you" and being willing to request "Please forgive me."

Christian marriage forms a circle of love that gathers in the whole family, speaking words of appreciation, demonstrating gratitude, teaching godliness, having the capacity to forget and forgive.

Marriage is more than just marrying the right person. It's being the right partner — united in love for a lifetime through God's wondrous gift of marriage.

The bond between a husband and wife grows strong through small acts of kindness, love, and consideration. Like mortar between bricks, open communication cements the marriage relationship and creates a bond that cannot be broken.

4

C h a p t e r

God's Design for
the Bedroom

*. . . Let us love one another, for love
comes from God. . . .*   — 1 John 4:7

*D*o you realize that God created sex?

That's right. It's not something that Galileo
or Copernicus or Sir Isaac Newton discovered. It's
not something Thomas A. Edison invented.

It is a creation of Almighty God.

Historically, Christian leaders have paid little
attention to the sexual needs and problems of the
flock. In fact, it is quite possible to go to church for
a lifetime and find the only recognition given to sexu-
ality is the occasional baby dedication.

Sex is a key part of our lives, and it is time to stop pretending it doesn't exist.

The Bible teaches us that sexual intercourse is a very special act, even a sacred act. It was designed for two people who have entered into a sacred covenant called marriage.

Husbands and wives are members of the most important organization on the face of the earth. Why? Because a marriage, working with God, creates immortal creatures.

Think about that.

God ordained that out of this incredible act called "sex," humans should have the ability to create everlasting life. When a man and a woman cause a new life to come into being, their child resides on earth for whatever term God has ordained — but then lives on eternally after his or her time here on earth is over.

We humans can produce little versions of ourselves, complete with souls that live forever. Next to eternal salvation this is the greatest gift in the universe.

God gave us sex for another reason — love. The purpose of sexual union is to express love for our spouse.

God *is* love. God does not have love, God *is* love. God *has* power, but God *is* love. The essence of God is love. If anyone ever discovers love, he has discovered God because God is the very essence of love.

Love has to be expressed in order to live. Love cannot be locked up in a golden box and put on a shelf. If love does not function, and if love does not express itself, it ceases to be love.

God gave us sex to express that love. God intended that sexual intercourse be used only by two people who have entered into the covenant of marriage. Each time a husband and wife come together in sexual union they renew the marriage covenant — a recommitment of the faith, love, and trust vowed when they were pronounced man and wife.

One of the most important aspects of sexual intercourse within marriage is that it can allow us to know and be known in a way that verbal intercourse can never do. When compared to any other activity in which we engage, sex allows us to share a greater degree of giving and receiving.

Another important aspect of sex in a marriage relationship is that sex is not an option, it is a requirement.

Why did God make marital sex an obligation? It has to do with how He made us and how He designed marriage.

God's Plan for Sex

Some Christians would like me to say that sex is depraved. It can be, but that is not how God designed it to be.

Lust is a disordering of God's plan for sex.

In our sex-conscious society, lust can become a very powerful force leading people to become sexually aggressive and selfish. It causes them to use others as objects — impersonal tools for sensual pleasure.

Even in marriage, there are restrictions regarding sexual behavior. Ephesians 5 and 1 Corinthians 13 make it very clear that marital relations are to be consensual.

No marriage can be strong if one partner does not care whether the needs of the other are met. Nor can a relationship grow when one partner is terrified of the sexual intentions of the other.

Within marriage, lust can cause a mate to be entirely selfish and only interested in self-satisfaction. In its worst forms, lust leads to fascination with pornography and sexual entertainment.

"Perfect love casts out fear," according to 1 John 4:18. The opposite can also be true — fear can cast out love.

It goes without saying that we need the help of God to overcome any sort of temptation. God's Word promises that we will have His strength when we need it to enable us to overcome sexual temptation.

Some marry because they need a mate to fulfill their sexual wants and desires. Is that wrong? Not at all. First Corinthians 7:8-9 mentions no other reason to get married. Of course, other verses throughout the Bible do. The entire book of the Song of Solomon is filled with romantic love poetry.

"Now to the unmarried and the widows I say: It is good for them to stay unmarried, as I am. But if they cannot control themselves, they should marry, for it is better to marry than to burn with passion" (1 Cor. 7:8-9).

If you are burning with lust, unable to restrain

your passions, and filled with uncontrollable passions, you should get married, according to these verses. After all, God recognizes that He designed us with a built-in need for each other.

Can those urges be resisted? Absolutely. First Corinthians 7:1-2 couldn't be much more plain, particularly when considered in the context of 1 Corinthians 7:8. Those verses tell me that the life of a single-minded Christian evangelist is far easier without family obligations: "Now for the matters you wrote about: It is good for a man not to marry. But since there is so much immorality, each man should have his own wife, and each woman her own husband" (1 Cor. 7:1-2).

However, 1 Timothy 4:1-4 tells us that men who forbid believers to marry are listening to the doctrines of devils.

> The Spirit clearly says that in later times some will abandon the faith and follow deceiving spirits and things taught by demons. Such teachings come through hypocritical liars, whose consciences have been seared as with a hot iron. They forbid people to marry and order them to abstain from certain foods, which God created to be received with thanksgiving by those who believe and who know the truth. For everything God created is good, and nothing is to be rejected if it is received with thanksgiving, be-

cause it is consecrated by the word of
God and prayer.

These verses indicate the Lord realizes that
even the most dedicated Christian faces temptations,
so "let every man have his own wife, and let every
woman have her own husband."

Within the confines of marriage, they are supposed to submit unselfishly to the other's needs.

"The husband should fulfill his marital duty
to his wife, and likewise the wife to her husband"
(1 Cor. 7:3). This verse proclaims that the husband
is supposed to give his wife her conjugal rights and
that the wife must give the husband his.

Notice that the woman is mentioned first in
that verse. The husband is supposed to give her the
rights that are hers. Then, the verse adds that the
woman is supposed to give the man his rights, too.

According to 1 Corinthians 7:4-5, after a
couple is wed, the wife no longer has the right to do
as she pleases with her own body. She no longer has
sole authority over it. She cannot claim it as hers
alone. It is also her husband's!

And it works the other way around, too. The
husband's body also belongs to his wife.

> The wife's body does not be-
> long to her alone but also to her hus-
> band. In the same way, the husband's
> body does not belong to him alone but
> also to his wife. Do not deprive each
> other except by mutual consent and

for a time, so that you may devote yourselves to prayer. Then come together again so that Satan will not tempt you because of your lack of self-control" (1 Cor. 7:4-5).

So, the Lord tells us, restating for the sake of clarity in verse 5 what He already declared in verse 3: Husbands and wives must never withhold sexual relations from each other. They must not deprive each other. One must never refuse the other.

Why? Because our Almighty God did not make man and woman to control one another. He made male and female to complete each other. Because of His master design, we need each other. There is within each of us an emptiness that only the other can fill. That emptiness was put there by God for our good and for His glory.

Why was this passage written into the Bible? One reason, I believe, was to put into black and white that God does not consider sex between husband and wife to be dirty or impure.

It is required!

Marriage or Celibacy?

Bible scholars tell us that the Corinthian church had been influenced by Gnosticism, a false doctrine that emerged in the early days of the Church.

Gnosticism taught, among other things, that our physical bodies are inherently evil. Out of this absurd teaching came two heresies that were in total opposition to one another.

The first heresy held that our bodies are evil, so what you do with them makes no difference. They taught that you can do whatever you want with your body — get drunk, be a prostitute, be a glutton, or whatever, since our evil bodies do not matter, only our souls.

The other Gnostic heresy disputed that teaching but said that since our bodies are evil, they should be tightly disciplined. All appetites of the body, they believed, should be subdued, including sex.

Well, the Bible teaches that God made man and saw that His creation was very good. The Bible regards the material body as precious and significant, the temple of the Holy Ghost, according to 1 Corinthians 6:19. "Do you not know that your body is a temple of the Holy Spirit, who is in you, whom you have received from God? You are not your own. . . ."

In the sixth chapter of 1 Corinthians, the Lord inspired the apostle Paul to take a strong stand against the sexual looseness which the first group of Gnostics practiced. Then in chapter 7, we find that the Lord is equally opposed to unnatural abstinence, which the other group of Gnostics taught.

No marriage is intended to be non-sexual. I find it impossible to justify a non-sexual marriage biblically. There is no reason for any husband or wife to be ashamed of their sexual relationship.

I have been asked what to do if your partner, particularly the husband, appears to be disinterested.

My advice to that wife is — seduce him. It is perfectly legitimate since you have said, "I do." Stir his embers. Light his fire. There is no reason that you shouldn't. Nowhere does the Bible say anything to the contrary.

If any of you ladies have husbands who are roving husbands, there is one simple answer: Keep him tired.

Husbands, the same goes for you. Let your wife know that she is a desirable, wonderful gift from God.

Even after reading 1 Corinthians 7, some people still ask, "Should the unmarried marry?"

"Unmarried" means bachelors, women who have never wed, widows, widowers, and divorcées.

Was Paul recommending celibacy?

It certainly appears so. But he also seems to be saying that it is only for a few people.

Celibacy, I believe, is as much a spiritual gift as the gift of prophecy or the word of knowledge. Like every other spiritual gift, celibacy is not only given, but it has to be received. It can be refused just like the other spiritual gifts.

Medical studies indicate that being an unmarried male decreases your life expectancy by nine years and seven months. If these figures are right, that means a man could lose nearly a decade of life if he does not have a wife!

How to Treat the Opposite Sex

In American society today, nothing is sacred. Tabloid-style talk shows parade people involved in every imaginable form of sexual behavior before their audiences. Late-night TV comedians go to great lengths to make sexual jokes out of any and every common situation in life.

Sex should not be the subject of filthy talk, ribald jesting, indecent joking, dirty stories, or coarse buffoonery.

Such talk, according to Ephesians 5:4, is not befitting a Christian. It is beneath your holy calling and unbecoming to your character. "Nor should there be obscenity, foolish talk or coarse joking, which are out of place, but rather thanksgiving."

Sexual purity is required, proclaims the next verse. "For of this you can be sure: No immoral, impure or greedy person — such a man is an idolater — has any inheritance in the kingdom of Christ and of God."

That is pretty strong! The Lord has no place in His kingdom for the sexually impure. We are supposed to confine our sexual activities to our spouse.

The chapter goes on to warn us about our behavior in verses 6-7: "Let no one deceive you with empty words, for because of such things God's wrath comes on those who are disobedient. Therefore do not be partners with them."

> • We are not to let anyone mislead us on this topic with empty words and clever arguments.
> • This kind of behavior comes only from disobedient people in rebellion against the Lord.
> • We are not even supposed to associate with such people.

The chapter then goes on to talk about submission and sacrificial love.

Feminists accuse Christian men of being delighted with those verses, particularly Ephesians 5:22, which orders women to submit and subordinate themselves to their husbands. "Wives, submit to your husbands as to the Lord."

Why is it the woman who submits to the man? Why not the other way around? Well, I didn't make the rules.

However, 1 Peter 3:1-6 gives us insight:

> Wives, in the same way be submissive to your husbands so that, if any of them do not believe the word, they may be won over without words by the behavior of their wives, when they see the purity and reverence of your lives. Your beauty should not come from outward adornment, such as braided hair and the wearing of gold jewelry and fine clothes. Instead, it should be that of your inner self, the unfading beauty of a gentle and quiet spirit, which is of great worth in God's sight. For this is the way the holy women of the past who put their hope in God used to make themselves beautiful. They were submissive to their own husbands. . . .

First, the wife is once again instructed to submit to her husband — to fit in with the man's plans, rather than disrupting the family with her own separate agenda. Why? So that non-Christian husbands may be won to the Lord by the pure daily lives of their wives, their chaste behavior, their respectfulness, and their blameless conduct.

What about Christian husbands? Such submissive behavior makes a woman precious in God's sight and beautiful in the eyes of her husband, says verse 6.

Christian husbands are told in verse 7 that they are to conduct themselves toward their wives with understanding and consideration.

What follows is one of the most controversial passages of the Bible — a phrase that feminists despise. Verse 7 goes on to tell husbands that they must show deference to their wives because women are weaker than men.

This verse teaches that since women are the weaker sex, husbands must honor them and defer to them. Their weakness, however, does not keep them from being equal in the eyes of God. Instead, men are warned that they must remember that their wives are equal heirs of the grace of God.

That warning even has a penalty! Husbands must regard their wives as equals in God's sight so that nothing interferes with His hearing their prayers.

Treating your wife as a second-class citizen can halt your prayers from wafting heavenward! Mistreating your wife can result in heaven turning a deaf ear to your requests!

When my mother told me to be a perfect little

gentleman to girls, she was training me so that my prayers would not be hindered when I became a husband.

There is little point talking to God if you, as a husband, are not talking to your mate. You can debate with Him, argue with Him, threaten Him, do all the things we do in an attempt to get Him to do the things we want Him to do. However, he will remain indifferent to us husbands if we are not properly regarding and honoring the partner God has provided for us.

Subordinate But Not Inferior

Some people think that because Eve was made to help and serve Adam, that she was inferior to him. The Bible does not teach anywhere that women are inferior.

It does say they are supposed to be subordinate. Many Christian men have missed that point. Subordinate does not mean inferior.

Jesus is subordinate to the Father, but He is not inferior to Him. The Holy Spirit is subordinate to both the Son and the Father, but He is not inferior to them.

And a woman is not at all inferior to her husband, even though she is to be subordinate to him. She is just different, and I am glad she is.

Genesis 2:18 is sometimes read to mean that God said, "I will make a help mate for him." However, He said "help meet."

The word "meet" is an Old English term that means "appropriate to; suited for; and fitted to," and the word "help" means more than assistance — it means partner. The Lord was saying, "I will make a partner suited to and appropriate for him."

If any man considers himself superior to women, he has only to engage in one interesting and illuminating experiment — having a baby. Let me remind you that at no time in human history has a man ever fathered a baby without the participation of a woman.

There is one dramatic instance in human history, however, when a woman gave birth to a baby without having sex with a man. God used a submissive young woman as the vessel through whom He would bring the Saviour of the world. Throughout the centuries, Mary, the mother of Jesus, has been honored and revered for her selfless act of obedience to God.

Husbands, God expects you to revere your wife as a precious gift and treasure her as a priceless possession. As you show her how much you love her, your sex life will begin to fall into line with God's plan for your marriage.

The Other Person in Your Marriage

A Christian marriage includes more than just a husband and wife. There is another person involved in this relationship — God.

That may sound odd to you, but let me explain, using the illustration of our solar system, which includes the earth, our moon, and the sun.

You know that the earth travels around the sun, and the moon travels around the earth. The moon's orbit is controlled by both the gravity of the earth and of the sun. But the gravity of the moon also influences the orbit of the earth. So the moon and the earth have major and important influences over each other, yet both are dependent on the influence of the sun.

That is the way in which a husband and wife must relate to God. Like the sun, our God exercises a relationship over both the husband and the wife — individually and jointly. The wife influences her husband and his relationship to God. The husband influences his wife and her relationship to God.

The influence of the wife on the husband and the husband on the wife directly affects the relationship they have with each other. It also affects the relationship they have with God — provided that they have committed themselves to Him.

One of the greatest leaders of ancient Israel, Joshua, the successor of Moses, once proclaimed in Joshua 24:15, ". . . choose for yourselves this day whom you will serve. . . . But as for me and my household, we will serve the Lord." He knew that only by having God as the head of your home will your marriage prosper.

Most church weddings include within the ceremony a special time where the bride and groom make a public, solemn vow to place their marriage under the authority of the Lord Jesus Christ.

But for too many people, that's the end of it.

Nobody ever explains to the couple exactly what they are vowing, so once the honeymoon is over, the battle begins.

They didn't realize what it meant when they said Christ was Lord of their marriage. So, they have no idea what to do when it turns out that He isn't.

Not every Christian has made the commitment to "grow in the grace and knowledge of our Lord and Saviour Jesus Christ" (2 Pet. 3:18). Instead, believers often think that just by becoming a Christian, they have done everything necessary to be a top-notch church member.

Jesus Christ, however, expects much more. He wants to be your friend and your Lord. He expects you to mature.

Marriage demands increasing maturity in character, responsibility, and wisdom.

I challenge you to make this important commitment right now. With your lips and your heart, commit your marriage and your home — and your sex life — to Jesus Christ. Declare that He is Lord over everything.

Then, diligently, daily, seek Him for guidance and help. Ask the Holy Spirit to fill you and help you make it work — even if your spouse is not a believer. Your marriage can succeed if you fulfill your proper role and let your mate fulfill his or hers.

Staying Within the Lines

*Starting a quarrel is like breaching a
dam; so drop the matter before a
dispute breaks out.* — Prov. 17:14

The world in which we live maintains order through
established areas of authority. Governments, institutions, businesses, churches — all function under
strict chains of command in which different people
have certain levels of authority. Authority, however,
can be used properly or improperly.

At school, the teacher is the authority in
charge. If the teacher says, "Do your homework," a
child must obey or suffer the consequences of losing recess or getting a poor grade on his report card.

If, however, the teacher tells that young person, "Disobey your parents," then the teacher has overstepped his bounds and gone into another area of authority that doesn't belong to him. In that case, the child does not have to obey the teacher.

Parents have authority over their own children to train and discipline them in righteousness.

If, however, a parent says to his child, "Go out and get drunk. Go commit adultery. Have a good time," they don't have authority in that area. That authority doesn't belong to the parent because God's word is higher than the parent's.

Your employer has authority over you in things that relate to your work. If, however, he tells you to lie and cover up his dishonest practices or violations of company policies, he is exceeding his authority. He has no moral authority over you, and you do not have to obey him if he expects you to disobey God.

Every strata of human living has levels of authority — and so it is with a husband and wife. Each has limited authority in the position that God has placed them. If they try to assume authority that God did not give them, it will never work.

In the home, a man has God-given authority, but in that authority God doesn't expect him to act like a bull, knocking everybody down and kicking everybody over.

If a man says to his wife, "You cannot worship God," that is not his authority. She doesn't have to obey him.

But what should she do?

What a terrible choice! That's why a Christian should never marry a non-Christian.

I know I have authority in my home, but I never forced the issue and said, "Look, I'm the boss." Good leadership never has to assert its authority or declare, "You better obey me."

In our home my wife and I never one time discussed authority. In fact, I always agreed with what she did and didn't interfere in her areas of authority.

If she disciplined the boys when they were young, I would support her and say, "Do you want me to add one more swat? I'll give them another one and make it two if you like."

If she bought $200 worth of groceries, I didn't walk into the kitchen and demand an explanation. Preparing the meals and feeding the family was her area of authority, and I trusted her to do what she thought was best.

She had her areas, and I had mine. One of my responsibilities was handling the money and making sure she had enough for our family's needs. My wife accepted the fact that I handled our family finances and didn't interfere with my decisions.

As the head of our household, I also had the authority to determine where we were going to live, the house we were going to buy, and when we were going to move, and so forth. She understood that.

Even though I had that authority, I didn't use it. Instead, I discussed these matters with her and would ask, "What do you think of this house? Would you like to live here?"

My wife has traveled with me all over the

face of this earth. When I said, "Let's go live in the Philippines," she didn't say, "Oh, dear, they just got through with a war and the place stinks and there are holes in all of the houses." She never said a word except, "Is God calling us to the Philippines?"

I said I believed that He was.

She responded, "Then, let's go."

I didn't come in and say, "Hey woman, you're going to go with me to the Philippines. I'm going to drag you over there." I didn't have to say that. I had the authority because God had told me to go.

She had the authority to say, "Tell me a little more about it." And I did.

She said, "That sounds great to me. Let's do it." So we went to the Philippines as one person.

Authority is an understanding of what has to be done. After gathering all the facts and getting input from those involved, somebody has to make the final decision. That is why God established lines of authority in the home.

A New Level of Respect

As Christians, our desire is to examine the Bible as carefully as possible in order to know God's will and obey it. Only the Bible can offer a final solution to the chaos and confusion with which today's families are confronted.

In the creation account, we find men and women were both equally created in the image of God. Neither received more of the image of God than the other. So the Bible begins with the equality of the sexes. As persons, as human beings, as spiritual beings, standing before God, men and women are absolutely equal.

Despite this equality, in Genesis 2, we see that while Eve was Adam's equal, she was given a role to fulfill in submitting to him and being his helper.

Genesis 3:16 says the woman's "desire" will be for her husband, but he shall "rule" over her. A careful reading of Genesis 2:18-25 shows that God created the woman to support her husband and to be a suitable companion to him.

In addition, women were active in the religious life of Israel throughout the Old Testament, but only a few were leaders, such as Deborah in Judges 4.

In the New Testament, we observe that Jesus spent time with women and apparently enjoyed their companionship — in stark contrast to other men of His day. In the midst of the Greek, Roman, and Jewish cultures, which viewed women almost on the level with possessions, Jesus showed love and respect for women.

Jewish rabbis did not teach women, but Jesus not only included women in His audiences, but used illustrations and images in His teachings that spoke to their needs. While the Jewish Talmud said it was better to burn the Torah than teach it to a woman, Jesus taught women freely.

To the Samaritan woman at the well, Jesus revealed that He was the Messiah. He also discussed with her such important topics as eternal life and the nature of true worship. Jesus never took the position that women, by their very nature, could not understand spiritual or theological truth.

He also taught Lazarus' sister Mary and, when admonished by the other sister, Martha, pointed out the priority of learning spiritual truth even over "womanly" responsibilities like serving guests in one's home (Luke 10:38-42).

Though men in Jesus' day normally would not allow women to count change into their hands for fear of physical contact, Jesus touched women to heal them and allowed women to touch Him. He even allowed a small group of women to travel with Him and His disciples — apparently unprecedented at that time.

After His resurrection, Jesus appeared first to Mary Magdalene and sent her to announce His resurrection to the disciples. Jesus did that even though women were not allowed as witnesses in Jewish courts because they were all believed to be liars.

In Jesus' treatment of women we see how He raised their station in life and showed them compassion and respect in a way they had never known before. But Jesus still did not exalt women to a place of leadership over men.

None of the twelve Apostles were women. Even at the cross where most of the men had fled and the women remained faithful, Jesus did not dismiss His male disciples and replace them with women. He made a radical break with His culture in so many ways that surely — if it had been God's will — He would have put women in a place of authority.

In His treatment of women, Jesus demonstrated their equality and worth as persons, but He did not promote them to positions of leadership over men.

Equal But Not Identical

God created woman to complete man, which means that man was deficient in several key areas. He still is. It is a foolish man who does not know he should listen to his wife's intuitions and instincts. Often she feels things that cannot be explained.

A woman evens out a man's rough edges, putting feelings on his logic and mercy on his judgment. She hugs and cuddles a hurting child while the husband thinks a playful punch or a little hair tousling will convey sufficient affection. Children need a father's toughness and a mother's tenderness.

God created each of us to fulfill different roles. The husband takes responsibility as the leader in the marriage, according to 1 Corinthians 11:3, but his success depends on whether he can maintain a servant's attitude.

Obviously, a woman is not supposed to be her man's slave. She is to submit to her husband, not blindly, but in accordance with the Word of God.

Humanity has heaped centuries of rubbish on the altar of matrimony by degrading the wife's role as the submissive chambermaid. Many women have endured such circumstances silently in the interest of peace — to no avail.

The only way the arrangement can work is if both mates pledge themselves to be the servant of the other. Then there will be peace, equality, and true submission.

In the Epistles we discover the same two principles side by side — both equality and submission for women. Galatians 3:28 points out that the way of salvation is the same for men and women and that they are members of equal standing in the body of Christ.

The passages on spiritual gifts also make no distinctions according to gender. Such scriptural exhortations as 1 Peter 2:1-3, Hebrews 4:16, Hebrews 6:1, Ephesians 5:18, Galatians 5:16, and Philippians 2:1-5 address Christian growth and behavior — and are directed to men and women alike.

Throughout the New Testament and alongside these passages on equality, however, are also passages that make definite distinctions between what God desires of men and women.

The biblical picture is of a union filled with love and harmony where both partners are submitting to one another, where both lovingly sacrifice for the best interest of the other, and where the husband is the leader in a relationship of two equals.

Husbands and fathers are given primary responsibility for the leadership of their families including their children, according to Ephesians 6:4, Colossians 3:21, and 1 Timothy 3:4-5. Wives and mothers are urged to be "workers at home" in Titus 2:5. The home and their children are to be their priority.

The apostle Paul is completely consistent with Jesus in regard to women. Paul had a high regard for women and shared his labors for the gospel with many of them. But, like Jesus, he never appointed them to positions of authority over men in the home or the church. As active as women were in the Early Church, nowhere did Paul ordain them as elders.

Men and women stand as equals before God, both bearing the image of God himself without making one inferior to the other. God calls upon both men and women to fulfill roles and responsibilities designed specially for them in certain situations.

In fulfilling those God-given roles taught in the New Testament, women are not limited. They are reaching their fullest potential because they are following the plan of their own Creator and Designer. Only in obedience to Him and in His design will women truly be able, in the fullest sense, to give glory to God, according to 1 Corinthians 10:31.

My wife has always worked right beside me. I took her everywhere I went because we had common goals and objectives. We were both missionaries when we met, so it was only natural that we should continue our work after we were married. In the churches I pastored, my wife played the organ and sang solos.

We had a radio program for years, and the two of us worked together ministering on the air. She would open each program with a song, and then I would preach. Our roles were different, but each of us functioned according to our God-given abilities.

God created both men and women to be servants of God and of each other. The husband and wife are equal in dignity and worth, and they are to work together as joint heirs of the grace of God, according to 1 Peter 3:7.

Working Two Jobs

In millions of American homes today, the wife comes home weary, groaning at the condition of the house, irritated that now she has to prepare dinner. The husband also comes home weary, half-angry that the house is a mess, and irked that no meal is on the table.

The stage is set for a serious confrontation.

Why? Because he is making her do two jobs.

Instead of deciding to either cut back on their family's spending or else find a job where he can get enough money to support them at the present lifestyle, he dumps part of his responsibility on her. Then she has to leave the home, go earn part of the family income, come home exhausted, and cram her real job into the evening hours.

What happens to the children?

They are raised by strangers during the day, then ignored by their parents in the evening while father snores in front of the TV and mother fumes in the kitchen.

The truth is that their home and their children are being sacrificed on the altar of money and an extravagant lifestyle. In a situation like this, it is time to simplify, to cut back, and to do with a little less.

A marriage is in a downward spiral when the husband and wife want more things, more money, more pleasures. In doing so, they settle for second best with their children and their personal relationship with each other. In their misery, they will never have enough money to satisfy their hurts, their anxieties, and that gnawing feeling that something is not right in their home.

In today's society, the mother and wife faces terrible pressure. She wants to make a solid financial contribution to the family that will take some of the burden off her husband.

Many choose to work to boost the family income so the family can have a new mini-van instead of a used station wagon; expensive summer camp in the mountains instead of inexpensive day camp at the local YWCA; a bigger house; all the most stylish clothes; and certainly every new toy advertised on TV.

I'm not talking about single parents who work because they have no other way to support their children. They have no alternative, and are exempted from guilt — at least by me — because they are having to be both nurturing mother as well as bread-winning father to the children.

Such parents deserve praise and support.

Moms who have husbands with decent-paying jobs *do* have a choice whether or not to work.

Some women work because they've spent so

many years preparing for their profession as a doctor, lawyer, or teacher. Society pressures the American woman to be a liberated mother, but is that what God wants?

I talk all the time with women who feel they must work or they will lose their identity. I ask them which is more important — losing their identity or losing their family?

Mixed Feelings

Many girls have grown up over the last 60 years being indoctrinated in school that they have just as much right as a man to have a fulfilling career. Then their babies are born, and they feel that hormonal surge of protectiveness and a deep desire to be with their children — not at the office while strangers hear the child's first word and applaud their first step.

Such women face such terrible inner stress. They are at odds with their desire to "be somebody," to use their minds, and to accomplish the tasks they are trained and educated to do.

A mother is chained by her love for her children, by her desire to see and participate in their growth, and by her fear for their safety when they are out of her sight. As a result, many mothers settle for a sad, confused mish-mash of working, suffering terrible guilt for not being at home, and watching their children growing older rather than being nurtured and held close.

I hear mothers trying to sort out their feelings all the time.

They feel pressured to work, but when they're at work, they can't get their minds off their children. Then, when they're with their children, they can't take their minds off the office. It is particularly stressful if the mom is an up-and-coming junior executive under intense pressure to give her all for the good of the company.

Many mothers admit having mixed feelings about leaving their children every morning for jobs that are not vital for family necessities. Young women are seeking career development as positive growth for themselves, but when they marry and have children, they are terribly torn.

Being a working mother is tremendously stressful.

Moms who have jobs outside of the home constantly fear that their children are not being appropriately supervised and their needs are not being met. Anybody who has ever raised a toddler knows that the child looks around about every three minutes to see where his mother is.

Knowing mom is close by is part of the child's sense of security. When such a child is dropped off at a babysitter, the mother and child lose that closeness. They need each other.

I see so many stresses on children today. Their days are manipulated to accommodate their parents' work schedules as well as activities such as school, homework, sports, and lessons, as well as pre- and post-school care. There's so little time for relaxation.

Children need their parents to be there for them when they return from school, to drive them to baseball practice or drama lessons, to take their temperature and feed them soup when they are sick.

I have only the highest praise for the man or woman who will turn down high-paying work if it means leaving their children alone for long stretches of time every day.

Finding Alternatives

After deducting from her paycheck all the additional expenses entailed by her working — maintenance of a second car, work clothes, convenience foods, and child care — even a well-paid woman clears very little at the end of the month.

Families need to count the costs, and not just the income, of a second job. When a mother has to contribute to the family income, she might do better — both financially and emotionally — to think creatively of alternatives to the standard 9 to 5 job.

The challenge for a mother who wants to combine child-rearing with income-producing work is that she may have to create a job for herself instead of hoping to find one ready made. She needs to ask questions such as: Can I negotiate a part-time position or job-sharing? Would a company consider flexible hours or take-home work? Can I free-lance from my home? Do I have skills that I can parlay into a home-based business?

Creative work arrangements can allow even single and low-income mothers to raise their own children.

I know of a woman who was divorced and working full-time when she began to feel that her children were being negatively affected by their separation from her all day. She used her experience as an English professor to create a home-based business as a book editor, which enabled her to be home with her children.

Another woman faced a life of dead-end jobs as a low-income single mother until she learned how to turn her love of art into a marketable skill. Now she makes hand-painted clothing at home, which she sells through several big-city stores. Her daughter helps by modeling her products.

Mothers who work at home are in a unique position to shape their children's values. Many children today never see their parents except during leisure hours. They have no role model of working adults with whom they can identify.

Children of home-based workers, on the other hand, actually see their parents meet deadlines, manage finances, and wrestle with decisions. They have the opportunity to learn from their parents the values and attitudes appropriate to the work world.

Working at home isn't just for mothers.

I know a man and wife who were both working full time when they decided the stress of balancing work and family was too great. His wife persuaded her employer to create a part-time position so she could be home more. The husband began to work from home as a consultant. Now he can adjust his schedule to attend his children's school functions or sports events.

Futurist Alvin Toffler, in his book *The Third Wave,* predicts that the next era of Western culture will be characterized by decentralization of the work place and a proliferation of home-based employment. Mothers and fathers who start now to create alternatives to the 9 to 5 work day while their children are young will be ready for that coming era.

Who Holds the Purse Strings?

In many marriages, there is much contention over who controls the purse strings. The working wife says, "I want to buy so-and-so, and I make more money than you do, so I have a right to it."

Many husbands and wives haven't been taught their proper relationships — especially when it comes to money. The cause of many divorces is related to money and career issues.

In millions of homes, the husband has his own bank account and the wife has her own bank account. When the bills are due, they go 50-50 to meet the expenses.

In doing this they are not living as one flesh, sacrificing one for the other as God intended. Instead, they are each remaining separate and independent — able to pull up their roots at a moment's notice.

When a husband makes money and puts it in the bank, his salary belongs to the whole family. It doesn't belong to him. If the wife makes money, it should also go into a common bank account.

My wife and I were married for a long time. If she needed money, I was always glad to give it to her. Never once did I ever say to her, "What did you do with that money?" It never crossed my mind to ask her.

Why? Because she was faithful with money.

As a result, if she wanted money, it was available to her without question. She didn't have to go out and work. That is my role. I am the breadwinner.

Where Your Heart Is

Money is a critical issue for many Christian families because it exerts such a powerful pull on the human heart. In the Sermon on the Mount, Jesus spoke directly to the rivalry between money and heaven. He told us in Matthew 6:19-20: "Do not store up for yourselves treasures on earth, where moth and rust destroy, and where thieves break in and steal. But store up for yourselves treasures in heaven, where moth and rust do not destroy, and where thieves do not break in and steal."

The world lies to us and says that money will buy us security, power, freedom, identity, pleasure, and happiness. It is true, but it lasts only for the moment. Money can't make anyone rich in the things that count for eternity. Spiritual blessings cannot be purchased with money, according to Acts 8:18-24.

In the Sermon on the Mount, Jesus preached to the hearts of the multitude gathered and wanted them to understand money's corrupting effects: "For where your treasure is, there your heart will be also," He warned them in Matthew 6:21.

Money promises us much, but it demands even more. It demands that we love it exclusively. "No one can serve two masters," Jesus warned us all in Matthew 6:24. "Either he will hate the one and love the other, or he will be devoted to the one and despise the other. You cannot serve both God and Money."

People who want to get rich fall into terrible temptations, according to 1 Timothy 6:9-10 and 17, which says that the love of money is the root of all evil. Some people, eager for money, wander from the faith and cause themselves terrible grief. They would do much better to put their hope in God.

Tithing is an Old Testament command that, simply put, required the ancient Israelites to give one-tenth of their income back to Him. In the Book of Malachi, all believers are actually challenged to "test God" as to His ancient promise that He will bless bountifully all those who obey Him.

I challenge you to try that test. Give to the Lord, and see what happens.

When you get your paycheck, look at how much is withheld. For every $100 you earn, the government takes its share.

I challenge you to start your own additional withholding system. As soon as you get your paycheck, immediately withhold 10 percent. Put it in the offering plate. Do not view the money as yours. Consider the tithe to be God's.

If you do, I can tell you right now that your financial situation is going to improve. You are going to see amazing things happen. You will be able to buy more with the remaining 90 percent than you ever did with the whole paycheck. It will just go further.

God teaches us to give freely and from the

heart. The New Testament teaches several other financial guidelines as well.

> • We are to give in response to
> need, according to Acts 4:35 and Acts
> 11:27-29;
> • We are to give in a systematic and purposeful manner, say 2
> Corinthians 9:7 and 1 Corinthians
> 16:2;
> • We are to give in a sacrificial
> way that "costs" us, according to Mark
> 12:41-44 and Luke 19:8;
> • We should always give in a
> secret and humble way, says Matthew
> 6:1-4;
> • And giving should be done in
> a cheerful manner, according to 2
> Corinthians 9:7.

Husbands and wives should pray together about every expenditure and every investment. They must be good managers — or "stewards" — at home and on the job. That's called "stewardship."

A married couple should mutually decide matters of finance, especially when large sums of money are involved.

Who's in Charge?

In a Christian marriage, we have all accepted that Jesus is Lord of our lives. That means He owns us. The apostle Paul went so far as to say that he was a bond servant — a slave — to Jesus Christ.

Well, if a slave lives in a house, guess who owns it? The slave owner does. If a slave is sold by his master, who gets to keep that house? The master. He can choose to sell the house along with the slave — but the choice is his, not the slave's.

So it is with us.

If we belong to Jesus, then everything we have is His. He is our provider. He is the one who has permitted us to have whatever we have. We are only caretakers of it.

It is that simple. We are managers of our resources for Him.

As such, we must be wise and careful. This also means that we have to be careful about how our money is spent and be obedient in giving our money according to God's guidelines.

With proper leadership functioning within a home, marital authority flows naturally. Both husband and wife know their respective roles and are content to fulfill them in a submissive attitude of give and take.

During our 49 years of marriage, Louise and I become so unified in directing our family affairs that we were unaware of who was actually in charge.

If asked, we both would have said, "It is Jesus."

A Package Deal

Honor your father and your mother,
so that you may live long in the land
the Lord your God is giving you.

— Exod. 20:12

When I got married, everything in my life changed.

Before, I had been a teenage evangelist, then a world-traveling missionary, mentored by a great man of God, a British evangelist named Howard Carter.

Once I got married, I couldn't just go off by myself anymore, I had a wife who went with me. I seldom went anywhere without her.

When we began to have children, everything changed again. I had to be there for them — not off somewhere on the other side of the world trying to save somebody else's children.

As our boys grew older, we returned to the mission field with our children in tow. When our mission work took us to Hong Kong and later to Israel, we took the boys along. We were a family — a package deal.

I believe that my sons learned lessons that would have been unattainable elsewhere.

Through our ministry in the Philippines they saw the power of the Lord at work. They saw first-hand what it is to depend on God for your next meal, for your rent, and certainly for doors to be miraculously opened so that the gospel can be heard by hundreds and thousands.

My children were a high priority in my life. When I came out of the church office at 5:00 p.m. and closed the door, I left all the problems of the ministry inside. If a problem tried to sneak out, I just kicked it in the behind and said, "Get back in there. You don't go anywhere. You stay here, and I'll be back tomorrow morning to take care of you."

If supper wasn't ready, the boys and I would go outside and throw the football around. Or, we'd take the basketball and put it through the hoop until my wife said it was dinner time.

After dinner, my wife and I both helped the children with their homework. She'd go to each of their rooms and see how this one was doing, and then the other. If they needed help, we were available to assist them. We gave them our full attention until they went to bed.

After they went to bed, if my wife and I wanted to talk or do something together, that was our time together. When it was the children's time, however, it was their time exclusively.

As a result, my wife and I were always really close to our boys, following precisely what they were learning, what they were doing, the kind of grades they were making. When necessary we visited the school and talked to their teachers. We did whatever it took to make sure our sons received a good education and participated in extra-curricular activities as well.

We considered our boys gifts from God and made sure they knew how special they were to us.

Lessons of a Madman

During one of the worst crises of his life, David was hauled against his will before the Philistine King Achish. In order to make his escape, David pretended to be insane. He acted in very degrading ways so as to give the impression that he had completely lost his mind.

He was driven away from the palace, and there in the street, a number of street urchins gathered around him, mocking him. He could not give up his pretense, so he had to endure them. That incident, however, taught him something very important.

Later in his life, he would sing songs of praise to God, remembering how he had become the laughingstock of little children. He sang about how he caused the future generations to think less of him because of his foolishness in the streets in front of the children. It inspired him to endeavor to undo the mischief.

"Come, my children," he sang in Psalm 34:11, "listen to me; I will teach you the fear of the Lord."

I believe that if David had never been in such a position, he would never have realized his duty to teach the little street children.

As king, he had the worries of the nation pressing upon him — the military woes, the political intrigues, and challenges to his authority from within his own household. I don't think he paid very much attention to the education of the street youth.

After being thrust into a position of having to pretend to be a madman, he saw all the little ruffians running wild and realized his responsibility as king of Israel to teach those children.

The Bible has many things to say about children.

God is also explicit in how we should raise children and what obligations grow out of love for our offspring.

A Simplicity of Faith

Psalm 127:3 states plainly, "Behold, children are a heritage from the Lord; the fruit of the womb is a reward" (NKJ). That verse should make mothers and fathers shout for joy!

When you see a little guy who looks exactly like you, reaching out his arms for you, it fulfills a need in the parent that nothing else can. Children are an amazing and wonderful blessing in the home.

I have heard many parents say, "You know, we're so happy that we have a child."

A child adorns a home with joy and brings much happiness. This is especially true of children who are raised in a Christian home. "They are always generous and lend freely; their children will be blessed" (Ps. 37:26).

Children are funny and bring many hours of laughter. You can't live with children and not find yourself laughing. That's one reason that they fill a home with such joy.

I came from a family with seven children, and I wouldn't give up my experiences in our home for anything in the world. I especially look forward to spending eternity with my brothers and sisters. We are going to be quite a bunch!

Children are a precious gift, and we have a sacred obligation to teach them about God. I believe there is no truth found in the Word of God which a child, if he is old enough to be saved, is not capable of receiving.

"Train a child in the way he should go, and when he is old he will not turn from it" (Prov. 22:6).

Jesus rebuked His disciples when they wanted to drive off the little children. "Let the little children come to me, and do not hinder them, for the kingdom of heaven belongs to such as these" (Matt. 19:14).

On another occasion, Jesus said, "See that you do not look down on one of these little ones. For I tell you that their angels in heaven always see the face of my Father in heaven" (Matt. 18:10).

Children can understand the Scriptures. In fact, children are capable of understanding some spiritual truths in early life that adults hardly understand in later years — such as faith.

Children have a simplicity of faith. There is little difference between the simplicity of a child and the genius of the profoundest mind. He who receives ideas simply, as a child, will grasp truths of God that a man who is prone to use deductive reasoning could never discover.

As soon as a child is capable of understanding the difference between right and wrong, he is capable of grasping the salvation message. As soon as a child can sin, that child can believe and receive the Word of God.

Never assume your children cannot understand spiritual matters. Use simpler words more fitted for their capacity and you can turn a little child from youthful lusts. Never treat the godliness of a young child with suspicion. It is a tender plant — nurture it, water it and you will be amazed at how it will bloom.

A Father's Character

In the story of the Prodigal Son a man had two sons.

The younger said to the dad, "Father, give me my portion of the inheritance. I'm going to leave. I don't like this place. I don't want to stay around here."

The father replied, "Well, if that's what you want," and gave the young man his portion of the inheritance.

The boy went to a foreign city and wasted the money on sinful pleasures. Pretty soon it was all gone, and he had nothing left. He found himself feeding pigs.

He said, "I don't like pigs. They stink, and I wish I wasn't here."

Then he realized, "My father's servants are better off than I am. I'm going to go back home."

He headed down the road to his father's house. As soon as he saw him, the father ran to meet him and forgave him for his waywardness and for wasting his money. He even gave the prodigal a ring and a coat and a welcome banquet.

The older brother, dismayed by the father's generosity, complained, "I stayed home and worked for you, and I haven't had a banquet."

The father said, "Now listen, son, I want you to know something. This is just to welcome your brother back home. All that I have left is yours" (Luke 15:11-32).

What does that mean? The prodigal who had squandered his own inheritance would not receive anything more. He got a ring, a coat, and a dinner, and that was it.

He had already received his inheritance, and he lost it through rebellion. By coming home, he was able to become a member of the family again. But the remainder of the inheritance totally belonged to the elder son who stayed at home.

The prodigal son was forgiven, and he was loved immensely. But he did not get a second chance at dad's money. He got what was coming to him.

The father in the story of the Prodigal Son carried through on his promise. Why is this important? Let me explain.

I am certainly no fan of Sigmund Freud, but in one of his early papers, he made a profound observation. He observed that the way his patients viewed God's characteristics was usually similar to the way they viewed their own biological father's characteristics.

Some patients, as children, had fathers who had threatened to punish them for wrongdoing but did not carry out the punishment. These adult patients held the strong belief that God would not condemn them either — but would always give them one more chance.

Others, whose fathers always carried through with the punishment, told Dr. Freud that they believed God always does what He says He will do, too.

That is the way the Bible describes God's character. God always carries through on His promises.

In Genesis 2:16 and 17, God stated what would happen if Adam and Eve ate the forbidden fruit.

In Genesis 3:14-24, He did what He said He would do. His promise of punishment was fulfilled when Adam and Eve were thrown out of the Garden.

Carrying Through

The most common mistake parents make is

that they do not carry through on their promises. A child soon catches on.

Let's say you tell him to be home at 2:00 p.m. or else he will be grounded for a month. When he doesn't come home until 6:00 p.m., you do nothing about it.

Next time, you tell him to be back by 2:00 p.m., and he comes home at 8:00 p.m. — if he feels like it. Or it may be 2:00 a.m.

If you say, "I'm going to punish you if you do such-and-such," then you let the child off, he will cease to respect you.

One way that you can keep this from happening is for both parents to solemnly pledge to carry through on their promises. The dad must carry through on the mom's promises, and the mom must keep the dad's word. To make discipline work, a husband and wife must be in unity.

What do I mean by that? They must be in harmony — in agreement.

Never once did my wife ever tell one of our boys, "Never mind what your father said — let me tell you the way it really is."

She never held their hand and said, "If he makes you clean up your room again, I'll get him back for you."

That kind of thing did not happen in our family. Our boys knew my wife and I presented a united front. That eliminated a lot of insecurity for them and avoided a lot of tension in the home.

If a child ever learns that he can divide Mom and Dad, then the home becomes a war zone with the child fighting all authority and seeing which parent he can get on his side.

Parental authority is also undermined when only one parent gets stuck with all the correction.

Never once did my wife ever tell our sons, "When your father comes home, I'm going to tell him about you, and he will spank you."

She took care of it herself — right then. She didn't wait for me to come home. When they needed discipline, she gave it to them.

We agreed together on our discipline, but we never hurt our children. If I spanked them on the behind, it was usually with my own hand. Still, they would yell as if I were killing them.

Children learn quickly what works with a parent. They will yell bloody murder as if you have injured them for life. If, at that point, you back away, believing their dramatics, they learn that the best way to get out of being punished is to be loud.

It never worked with me. I spanked them and when I was finished, I would say, "You can kiss me now." And I would give them a big hug.

"Now," I would ask, "do you think I did the right thing?"

And every time they would say, "Yeah, you did the right thing."

Then I would say, "Now, part of the discipline is for you to go to bed."

Some people may think that's not much of a punishment. All I know is that it worked, and my wife and I didn't have a lot of trouble with our boys. I told them what I would do if they broke the rules, then I always carried through.

Proverbs 19:18 says, "Discipline your son in his early years while there is hope. If you don't you will ruin his life."

Brothers and sisters, that's plain speaking!

It's vitally important to understand the consequences of failing to discipline our children. Proverbs 23:13-14 tells us what can happen: "Do not withhold discipline from a child; if you punish him with the rod, he will not die. Punish him with the rod and save his soul from death."

A Father's Heart

A father with a strong-willed teenage daughter sat down and wrote this note to her. It gives insight into what it takes to be a Christian parent.

Dear Angel,

I am sorry that you are upset. Believe it or not, it doesn't make me feel good at all when you feel badly. You're an important member of this family and when you hurt, I hurt. That's part of being a family. When one of us is in trouble, all of us feel it to varying degrees.

You see, believe it or not, I love you very much.

You are very important to me — and will be forever.

Last night, you basically told me to shut up when you were arguing with Mommy. You told me that you had not asked for my opinion. I told you that I do not need for my 13-year-old daughter to ask my opinion for her to get it anyway.

Things went downhill from there. I told you that if you stomped out of the room while I was talking to you, you would be punished by having to write 200 sentences about respecting your parents. You went through the door anyway — then wanted to argue that going into the hallway is not "leaving the room."

The argument continued with my asking you how many sentences you thought were fair. You shouted that you wanted to write 500, then 1,000, then 2,000 sentences. I halted things there and told you that it was a deal and that you were grounded until you finished your 2,000 sentences.

So, now, we have a problem. How on earth are you going to finish 2,000 sentences? How can I let you off and keep your respect? If I just let you off, then you will never believe that I mean business.

So, what do we do?

It would be very bad for you not to think that your father means business. I believe I am supposed to be very involved and very interested in you and, particularly, your development into a happy, productive adult. When I see a problem with one of my children, certain father-type instincts kick in and I set about finding a solution. That's just something that fathers do. I do not always find the right solution, but with God's help, I keep at it until I've done the right thing and the problem is correctly addressed.

I know that I need to help you develop spiritually — so our family has sought out the right church where that will happen. I also try to be a good example at home and teach you spiritual things.

It is my job as your father to help you be ready for adulthood. In about six years, you will be a legal adult. It is my job that when you turn 18, you will be ready to make the right choices to lead a happy, successful life within God's plan for you.

You will probably make some mistakes. Everyone does.

That's why my commitment to you will not end when you turn 18 and I could just cut you loose legally. Sorry, but emotionally, you will always be my little girl. When you are 59 and I am 87, I will still be there for you — probably telling you that your rich banker husband is an old fuddy-duddy and that you should have been nicer to the preacher's son.

This loving letter goes on with the father offering to let his daughter choose between a list of jobs around the house and conducting 10 interviews with adults so she can write short essays on the subject of how they learned to control their tongues.

The father who wrote that letter prayed the evening before writing it that the Lord would help him better communicate with his fiery-tempered little girl.

When he handed it to her, she bristled. But her attitude softened as she read the words that the Holy Spirit had led her father to write especially to her. That letter showed her his love.

This father knows that a home does not just happen. It requires hard work and necessitates intervention by parents.

The Holy Spirit is absolutely vital in this process. In our own human wisdom, we cannot always do the right thing — particularly when it comes to raising children. However, if we will pause and ask God to guide us through His Spirit within us, the results are always far, far better.

My Three Sons

My goal has always been to build a team ministry with my three sons. To do that, I knew I had to give away some of my control and authority. I couldn't hold onto the reins and make every decision.

As the administrator of our ministry, Stephen manages the personnel, signs all the checks, and pays the bills. When documents come in of a legal nature, I have Stephen check them over. Whenever I am out of the country, I know the ministry is in good hands.

My youngest son, Peter, is vice president and chief operations manager of all the TV and radio stations. His expertise in that area is a gift, and knowing he's in charge lifts a tremendous burden from my shoulders.

Frank, the oldest of my sons, co-pastors the church in South Bend with me. Our congregation loves him — he's full of joy and has the gift of evangelism. His pastor's heart often leads him to seek out the lost or to pray with those who are in need of comfort or healing.

Frank and my second son, Stephen, are both excellent preachers of the gospel. Often, when I'm listening to a tape of one of their sermons, something they say will jolt me into a realization of God's goodness or will send me searching God's Word.

Where did they get that from? I wonder, and *Why didn't I see it first?*

Today, many young people, who rise like a rocket in ministry, come down very early in life and are never able to reach the same height of blessing, anointing, or achievement again.

My sons have avoided that experience because the Lord trained them on the job just as He had done with me. I think that's why all three of my sons have been able to find their callings within our family ministry.

When they were participating in Manila, Hong Kong, and all the other places that they accompanied me, God was preparing them. By including them in every phase of the ministry, my sons knew they weren't just tagging along. Even at the age of 12 or 15 they were competent and responsible — no one ever called them greenhorns.

From the beginning, my sons knew that our ministry was their ministry, too. That's why today I can call on them to make important decisions.

Sure, there have been times when one of them has made a poor judgment call, but I just lean back and ask myself, *Let me see, he is 21 years old. When I was 21, what kind of decisions did I make?*

Then, I smile and say to my son, "Son, you made a good decision."

We can't always judge our children from our maturity and age level. We have to remember that they are only 5 or 10 or 12. We can't judge their decision-making from our level alone. Instead, we have to consider where they are in life.

Investing in the Future

After our boys grew up and left home to start families of their own, we still remained close. Louise and I would often go over to their homes for dinner and have fellowship with them.

If you are going to have a happy home, you've got to work at developing a lasting relationship with your children.

When our boys were very young, they talked all the time and all at the same time about three different things. At our dinner table, as they were growing up, my wife and I would enjoy listening to what they said.

If one of them butted in on the other, we would be the referees, telling them not to interrupt — but to wait until their brother was finished talking.

Because we listened to them — and let them know that we wanted to hear what they had to say, our boys felt at home. We never said, "Shut up! I'm tired of listening to you." That was never said in our home.

Our children had total freedom of expression. Often what they said was childish rambling that didn't mean much, except to them. We found, however, that by always listening to them, they would bring their troubles, their heartaches, and their misunderstandings to us. They would do it because we had an open channel with them. We listened to whatever they had to say.

As a result, my sons and I remain friends.

I was determined not to make the mistakes that other men of God have made throughout history. One of the great judges of Israel, Eli, had irresponsible children who were a humiliation to him.

If you want your children to take care of you when you are old, you'll begin working on that when they are one hour old. If you wait until they are 15 or 16, they are not going to take care of you in your old age.

So, nurture them, and they will nurture you. It will be natural for them to meet your needs since you have been meeting their needs all their lives.

Do not think that the government will take care of you in your old age. That simply will not happen. It is your children's duty and privilege to provide a place for you.

Some of the precious people that I see in nursing homes often haven't had a member of their family visit them in months. Their children don't care what happens to them. How did they get to that point?

If you could go back a few years, you would probably hear these same parents saying, "Get out of here. You are in my hair. I wish you would get married and get out of the house."

Other parents, however, are desperate that their children will actually survive without them. So they sabotage their kids' ability to be independent by manipulating and controlling them long after they have achieved adulthood.

Love does not manipulate. Love does not control.

Love holds a young adult close, then lets him or her go, trusting that years of godly rearing will keep that child nearby — yet functioning as a productive, happy adult.

I am so proud of my boys. They still come and go in our home. Yet, each has his own home as well. We remain a happy family.

7

Chapter

Where to Add the Insulation

*"You call me 'Teacher' and 'Lord,'
and rightly so, for that is what I am.
Now that I, your Lord and Teacher,
have washed your feet, you also
should wash one another's feet."*
— John 13:13-14

*M*y mother was single-minded when it came to Jesus. She reared seven children, producing four preachers. What an accomplishment!

Although my dad was a hard worker and a good provider — a foundry worker in shipyards and train yards — he was not much of a nurturing father. He left the child-rearing to my mother.

She would begin the day with reading the Bible, and always at night she gathered us together before going to bed. She read the Word to us. When we could recite the books of the Bible in order or when we could quote the Twenty-third Psalm or recite the Ten Commandments, she gave us prizes.

She worked hard all day making a home — and she was always there for us. Sometimes it was her fervent prayers that put food on our table.

At times our family was bitterly poor, particularly when my father was out of work. A number of times we had absolutely nothing, but she would set the table and begin to thank the Lord for the meal that we were about to enjoy.

I remember as a boy thinking that she must be nuts — that the table was bare. But what an impression it made on my young spirit when someone from the church would drop by with a casserole or a basket of fried chicken, declaring that they were just in the neighborhood or that the Lord had told them to bring something over to us.

In today's terminology our family would have been called "dysfunctional." My dad was not a godly man. He usually did not come straight home from work — instead preferring to stop off at the places where ungodly men gather after a hard day on the job.

Defying my mother's determined efforts that ours would be a Christian home, he brazenly pursued the pleasures of sin until he was an old man.

My mother prayed 30 years for my father to

become a Christian. One time when my mother was interceding for my father in the early morning hours, she saw a vision of a lion walking up on the porch and straight through the front door. It crouched on the other side of that door as if it owned the house and was going to take over.

My mother said for half an hour she battled that demonic lion in the Spirit until it backed out and went away. Finally, she took authority over the devil and claimed my father's salvation. For years, she continued to walk in the victory she had won that night and would say in faith believing, "My husband is saved."

Her friends would scoff, "You know he's not saved. He's mean as ever."

"Yes," she would agree, "but God told me He is going to save him, so he's saved."

My mother took authority in the name of Jesus and won the victory. My father was the last person in our family to get saved, but my mother's faith prevailed. When he finally submitted to the Lord, Dad's salvation became so precious to him that he actually did some revival preaching.

It was my mother's spirituality that brought my father to the Lord and held our family together.

The Power of A Parent's Prayer

My mother prayed me into the ministry.

I would often hear her calling out my name and praying, "Lord, make Lester to be a preacher. We need a preacher."

As a little boy, I would say, "Oh, don't listen

to that woman. I just can't stand that. I don't want to be any kind of preacher."

But she persisted, and she got what she wanted.

When I was 17 years old, I was converted on my deathbed and became a minister of the gospel of Jesus Christ.

We have a slogan in this country that says, "The family that prays together, stays together."

My mother was a living testimony to that.

God wants you to be a good example for your children. You are the role model on which they will base their lives. If you pray, they will pray. If you try to follow the Lord in humility and sincerity, they will, too.

When my three boys were growing up, I prayed with them every night. Privately, I prayed that they would give their lives to Christ.

I didn't pray for their position in life. I didn't pray for God to make them preachers. My mother had done that to me, and I didn't feel led to make that decision for them. I told the Lord I would be happy if my boys became preachers, but all I wanted was children who would grow up to serve my God.

The Lord answered my prayer far beyond my expectations.

In 1 Kings 3:9-12, we are told that King Solomon asked the Lord for "a discerning heart to govern your people and to distinguish between right and wrong."

God answered his prayer in a mighty way, giving Solomon not only the discerning heart that he requested, but making him wiser than anyone else in the history of mankind!

The Lord has done this throughout history — and He will do it for you.

In Judges 10:9-15, the besieged people of Israel humbly asked the Lord to help them in their losing battle against the Ammonites. Israel confessed their own sin, then asked God to "Do with us whatever you think best, but please rescue us now."

Well, deliver them, He did. Not only did He give them protection, but He gave them supernatural courage and direction to defeat the vast Ammonite army!

That's what happened with me. I asked the Lord to lead my boys to be faithful Christians. In response, my Almighty Father gave me three right-hands who have stayed in my ministry, allowing it to achieve heights that one preacher could never do alone.

Furthermore, the Lord is now giving me incredible, godly grandchildren who are joining the battle beside me! And a magnificent nephew!

I am so blessed.

Teaching Your Children God's Way

As a young father, I realized that I was to show my boys the way to heaven and the way to God. That way, of course, is Jesus Christ. The Holy Spirit also convicted me to teach my sons the Bible, and not doctrine or denominationalism.

From my experiences in the ministry, I knew it was important to teach my sons to respect others'

Christian beliefs. Today we have too many people mocking the theology of other believers. Sometimes it's downright embarrassing the way Christians make fun of what other Christians believe.

I don't think God gets the joke. Instead, He is deeply grieved when He sees His sons and daughters ridiculing each other over what they are convinced the Bible says.

In addition, I believe He is even deeply *angered* when He sees supposed Christians harshly denouncing other believers. I have seen in the lives of too many harsh critics the bitter fruits that come when you blast other Christian leaders.

Disagreeing is one thing, but ridiculing is wrong. Denouncing a fellow follower of Jesus Christ over theological differences is an abomination before the Lord. It gives ammunition to the enemy. It makes us a house divided — which, of course, cannot stand.

I don't think anybody should criticize another Christian. If you don't think someone's Christianity is correct, then you can either leave it alone or deal with it in a spiritual way.

You can show them Scriptures that you think refute what they believe and say privately to them, "Would you explain this to me, please?" Discuss their response. Let the truth defend itself.

Guess what? You may be wrong!

At one time in my life I trembled before the Lord, pleading with Him not to make me one of those crazy preachers who go around casting out demons. I wanted to have dignity in the pulpit and be respected. I did not care to be branded as a demon-chaser! I thought those guys were nuts.

God had something else in mind and humbled me in a mighty way. He gave me a special anointing to deal with Satan's evil oppressors. He gave me power over demons whether I liked it or not.

So, I caution you to remain humble before the Lord as you teach your children His ways. You may find that you have a lot to learn. I learn new things constantly.

Don't teach your children to use their Bibles as clubs. The Word is a mighty sword with which we pierce the enemy. It should not be used, however, to bop other believers in the head.

The Bible is not a book that we tear to pieces every day by quarreling and fighting. It's God's light and truth and power. All that is required of you is to read it and believe it — and live it before your children.

What's Most Important?

Spiritual training within the family is critical to the survival of civilization — not to mention our kids' eternal destinies. Certainly your kids' spiritual education is more important than their school work!

"Teach religion and have prayer in school," pleaded British parents in a recent National Opinion Poll. It showed that 58 percent of parents preferred that their children receive a religious rather than a non-religious moral education.

Interestingly, only 20 percent were interested

in inspiring their children's faith. The majority of others recognized that humanistic morality is failing: 36 percent endorsed teaching about God and prayer because they wanted their children to have a legitimate moral code; 38 percent wanted prayer and godly teaching to give their youngsters a proper base in history and culture.

British parents also regard religious education to be more important than music or art instruction. About 46 percent of those asked by *The Independent* newspaper said they thought the Bible should be taught as truth, and 70 percent told the newspaper they wanted prayer in the classroom.

At one time, America had Bible teaching and prayer in its schools. For 160 years our leaders protected and preserved our nation by mandating such instruction. Then, God was thrown out of America's public schools. The results make their loud, violent witness all around us.

How much emphasis does your family put on spiritual education?

I challenge you to get out a pencil and paper and jot down the number of hours that your children spend in school each week — probably about 30 hours. Add to that the time they spend on homework, and your child is probably devoting 35-40 hours a week to school studies.

Now, add up the time they spend weekly on athletics. I would guess that at the height of the basketball season, we're talking about 10 hours a week at practice and another two hours a week for competition — that's 12 hours weekly.

Now, how much time does your child spend in front of the television? I know some families whose youngsters plop down in front of the idiot tube as soon as they get home from school, then do not budge except for meals and bedtime. On weekends, it is the same story.

Let's say that your family regulates TV viewing to two hours a day. That's 14 hours a week. Probably it is closer to four hours a night and six hours on weekends. That would be 32 hours a week.

Now, how much time is devoted to your child's spiritual education? Sunday school would be one hour. Sunday morning church is another hour. Does your child go to Sunday evening youth meeting? That's another hour. If you stay for evening services, then come back on Wednesday night, that's another two hours. The total — and this would be a very faithful family: five hours.

Let's say that you also spend a half-hour every evening teaching your children about the Lord. That's another three and a half hours. The total? Eight and a half hours of spiritual training.

Is something wrong here? How can we be raising up a Christian generation when their spiritual education comes in a poor fourth place to school, athletics, and TV?

Humble faith in Jesus Christ is the insulation that protects a devout family from the evil outside forces. I believe it holds civilization, society, and the home together.

It brings a closer love between the husband and the wife and between the parents and the children. Teach your children to worship in your home, and teach them to pray.

On your refrigerator, put up two posters. On one, put prayer requests. On the other, record prayers when they are answered. This visual testimony of God's provision will strengthen your children's faith.

Show them how our great, loving God answers prayer. Witness to them about what God means to you. Encourage them to take everything to Him — and to rejoice when He answers.

When your family faces a crisis, include the children in your prayer time as you ask the Father to provide your needs and deliver you from harm. As a result, they will learn how to pray in their own times of need and will have the faith to believe that God truly does answer prayer.

What Can a Parent Do?

As a parent, it is up to you to protect your children from the multicultural baloney being taught in their schools in the name of pluralism and cultural diversity. Make sure that Jesus Christ is real and alive to your children, not just an interesting person to study.

Two worlds are colliding in the classroom. At stake in the swelling battle are the hearts and minds of our next generation.

On one side are those who are deceived by Satan. That may sound strong, but a passive humanist who doesn't see the need for any kind of moral training is headed straight to hell just as surely as the wild-eyed satanist who is guilty of ritual sexual abuse against innocent children.

On the other side is Christianity — the largest religious movement in the world. Today, there are 1.75 billion people who say they are members of the Christian religion — roughly 33 percent of the world's population.

Think what an impact Christians could make on our world if only we would raise our voices together in harmony to the Almighty. Our differences are so insignificant when compared with the evil, false religions enslaving millions.

Please don't teach your children to hate other Christians. Show them what the Bible really says about important issues, but don't teach them to hate anybody.

You should, however, caution your children about listening to the teachings of those who are deceived by Satan. Tell them to be skeptical and discerning toward any teacher who is not a Christian. Do your best to get your child into classes taught by believers — and certainly out of classes taught by anyone who worships a false god.

Teach your children to pray for their teachers and school administrators. Encourage them to pray that God will protect Christian teachers from the godless forces that boldly declare Christianity to be an enemy of public education.

The massive National Education Association has become increasingly bold in its attack against Christianity, and many Christian teachers are questioning their allegiance to this liberal organization.

"I belong to the National Education Association, but sometimes I feel like quitting," confesses educator Tom McLaughlin. "The NEA still doesn't realize America is fed up."

More accurately, the vast teachers' union does not care.

Asked at a news conference why the moral fabric of American society seems to be deteriorating, evangelist Billy Graham blamed lack of moral teaching, especially in schools.

We need Christian teachers to stay in the NEA and keep an eye on their rotten agenda. We certainly need Christian teachers to stay in the schools, quietly encouraging our children.

Remember that more than half of all Americans claim to be Christians. Only a very small minority profess to be atheists or pagans. Many people claim no faith, but we Christians are in the vast majority.

It is time we quit sitting back and letting militant enemies of Jesus Christ subvert our children's faith.

Your children need to know that they must have nothing to do with any religion that does not believe that Jesus Christ is the only way for mankind to receive eternal salvation.

Combating the Darkness

Certain militant, active forces within our government and in our schools — and certainly in the media — are intent on training our children in ungodly ways. Let me quote from a training sheet prepared by New Agers to help discredit Christianity:

There are some who wish to make biblical law the law of the land rather than the Constitution. Those who wish this are a vocal minority, even within the Christian faith, but they have positions of authority in the Christian subculture. These include men like Pat Robertson, Patrick Buchanan, D. James Kennedy, and Rousas John Rushdoony. While it might seem at first preferable to have biblical law running our seemingly out-of-control nation, keep in mind that there is much law in the Bible that is not even enforced on Christians. For example, misbehaving children, homosexuals, and those who violate the Sabbath could be executed under biblical law. Many of the laws in the Bible were written in a primitive time for primitive people. Would such laws work today?

Those who seek to "fix" society by resorting to the Bible for answers to social problems are about as useful as car mechanics who try to fix 1993 Corvettes with 1925 Ford Model T shop manuals. Our economics, politics, families, and social environments are far more complex than before. Teacher-led prayer, presenting creationism as if it were valid science, and putting the Ten Commandments on classroom walls will do far less for education than adequate funding, better facilities, smaller classes, and better pay and working conditions for teachers.

With the knowledge to argue intelligently with Christians plus the understanding that there are Christians who are not fundamentalists and are opposed to the idea of imposing the fundamentalists' regressive sociological views on American society (liberal Christians, in fact, fear that the fundamentalists' emphasis on the Bible is destroying Christianity), we can, at the very least, show that the 'evidences' for the inerrancy of the Bible are fictitious and that one can lead a moral, upright, and decent life without religion in general and the Christian fundamentalist religion in particular.[1]

How do you prepare your precious children to combat this kind of propaganda?

Teach them the truth. Put the Word of God in their hearts so that they will not depart from it. Tell them point-blank the absolute truth that Jesus is the only way to get to heaven, regardless of what movies, TV, and paperback books may tell them.

If you doubt that the entertainment industry

teaches a false gospel, then consider the hit movie *Ghost* in which the souls of bad people are sucked into terrifying darkness and nice folks' souls are greeted by a twinkling spotlight from the sky. The film ends with the hero, a soul stranded on earth, finally being greeted by the brilliant light — although in the two hours of the movie he never gives any hint that Jesus had any lordship over any part of his life. Instead, the ghost contacts his widow through a spiritualist medium, something that is absolutely forbidden in the Bible.

Especially around Halloween, your children may be exposed to all sorts of occult "games," including seances and Ouija board sessions, and group discussions about whether there really are such things as ghouls, zombies, goblins, and ghosts. Some schools even have real-live witches come into the classroom as guest speakers — "white" witches who practice the ancient occultic Wicca religion, and who delight in telling school groups that they only use their magic to do good.

Show your children the passages in the Bible that say all magic is evil (Lev. 19:31 and Deut. 18:9-14), that witchcraft is a sin that ranks right up there with murder (Exod. 22:18 and Gal. 5:20), and that Israel's King Saul's life was forfeited because he consulted with a witch (1 Sam. 28:7).

Your children also may be exposed in school to Zen Buddhist meditation or Hare Krishna chanting or Wiccan worship of earth spirits. More likely, they will be exposed to books and films that take a cynical attitude toward any religion, portraying believers as unsophisticated dupes of superstition and tradition.

Teach them that they can refuse to participate in any kind of non-Christian ritual — just as the Hebrew children Shadrach, Meshach, and Abednigo did growing up in pagan Babylon. And if you are feeling bold, tip off your school's principal that you just might haul into court anyone who discriminates against your children for their Christian faith.

Pray fervently that your children will stand tall when confronted by those who hate Jesus Christ. And pray that the Lord will provide your children with Christian friends or children open to learning about Jesus. There is nothing quite as exciting as leading a buddy to Jesus. It will build your child's faith dramatically.

Opposing Sides

In the world that we live in today, the tragedy that occurs when a Christian marries a non-Christian is quite prevalent. I have seen it time and again.

Here is a good rule. Don't let your child date anyone that they should not marry. Think about this: *Most people marry someone that they've dated.*

While your child lives under your roof, you are entitled to make the rules — which should include not dating anyone outside your religious faith.

Two opposing worlds are at war in any home in which one spouse is a Christian and the other is a non-Christian. In the throes of young love, such a marriage will be rocky, but they may make it work. After they have been married a while, and he says, "Let's go to the mosque," and she says, "No, let's go to the church," there will be friction.

When they have children, what is going to happen? One says they are going to be Muslim trained. The other says they are going to a Christian school. It's so important that there be a unity in spiritual things in your home.

What about a Baptist who marries a Methodist? The Methodist says, "I can tell you now, I don't want any deep water dunking for me."

The Baptist says, "Well, all you got was a sprinkle." They begin to make fun of each other's religion, and it brings friction that could ultimately tear them apart.

I mourn for any family that has to split up on Sunday mornings with the husband going one place to church and the wife going to another. The children don't know which place to go. Believing the same and worshipping the same is a lot simpler.

If your family is divided theologically, avoid arguing about religion in front of the children. Let's say that in your family one believes in the inspiration of the entire Bible. The other, however, says it is an imperfect document created by men. Keep your theological debates light, friendly, factual, and private. Never let them get personal or insulting.

Don't get mad. Religious disagreements can escalate in a home until the children don't have any respect for religion. You want them to have a high regard for things of God — not memories of both parents pointing out why the other parent's faith is foolish, false, or flaky.

Guidelines for Dating

Today's American culture puts tremendous pressure on young people to begin dating at an early age. But should you allow your children to date at all?

I would recommend encouraging young sweethearts to meet each other at church functions and school-sponsored athletic events. So much of Hollywood's entertainment these days is not suitable for Christian children.

Never permit someone more than a year older than your child to go out with your youngster. After age 17 or so, you might relax that rule, but closely monitor any wide age variances.

At what age should modern Christian children be allowed to date?

Before age 14: The only thing resembling a date should be a well-chaperoned public, group event — preferably church-sponsored — where your child arranges to meet their friend of the opposite sex. By well-chaperoned, I mean that you be prepared to stick around if there is insufficient adult supervision. Do not provide transportation for the other child. It will be much less of a "date" if the two just meet at a party, rather than arrive together. Have a 9:00 p.m. curfew.

Ages 14-15: Continue to stick around and permit group events only. For private parties, thoroughly check out the parents involved. You would be amazed at how many "good" parents allow alcohol to be served at junior high events. Do not allow situations in which the two youngsters are alone in a room together. Extend the curfew to 10:00 p.m.

Ages 16 and older: Encourage group events but allow occasional car dates, provided you have complete confidence in your child and their friend. If you don't trust your child, stick with group events and group transportation. What about the curfew? I would suggest 10:00 p.m. on school nights and 11:00 p.m. on weekends. For special events, extend the curfew to midnight. Why so early? Because your children need to be doing whatever they are doing in the light of day. The cover of darkness provides unnecessary temptation.

Why am I so restrictive? I know some parents are allowing their 10 year olds to go on completely unsupervised movie dates and permitting young teens to sit alone in bedrooms with doors closed. For that matter, some foolish parents are giving their 14 year olds condoms and telling them to be "responsible."

Well, such permissiveness is foolish. I feel it constitutes parental neglect bordering on abuse. Such a lack of supervision demonstrates complete disregard for a child. A loving parent is protective.

A caring parent says, "No."

It's Up to YOU

Only *you* can insulate your home against the worldly elements that will try to creep in through the woodwork. As the parent, you are held responsible by God for the ungodly influences you allow to come into your home.

It's up to you to take a stand. It's your responsibility to turn off the television when actors are taking the Lord's name in vain and spewing profanity into your living room. *You* have to monitor what your children watch. *You* have to set the standards for movies and videos and stick by them.

God expects *you* to know where your children are, what they are doing, and who they are with. If you don't care, who will? Believe me, I'd rather err on the side of being over-protective than to release control too soon and send my precious child out into an evil world that cares nothing about him or her.

Don't give up too soon. Keep fighting for your children because, believe me, a powerful enemy waits just outside your front door. He preys especially on children whose parents have bought the lie that children need freedom and independence in order to grow up. That's true to a point, but they also need your supervision and guidance.

When your children are away from you — with the babysitter, at school, in extra-curricular activities, with friends — your responsibility for them does not end. During those times, you can insulate them with prayer. Intercede for their protection and guidance and direction. Pray that they will have wisdom to know right from wrong and be able to discern the devil's schemes and resist temptation.

When your child has shown he can handle tempting situations and act responsibly when confronted by peer pressure, then you can release the reigns a bit and give him or her more freedom. You'll know when the time is right. At that point, your child should be able to build his own spiritual insulation around his heart and mind and spirit.

Think what a joy it will be when your child begins to exhibit mature Christian behavior and takes responsibility for his own spiritual walk with the Lord. Who knows? He might even start praying for you!

Notes
[1]*Christian Crusade Newspaper,* Neosho, MO, 1994.

8

Chapter

Following God's Blueprint

*He created them male and female
and blessed them. And when they
were created, he called them "man."*

— Gen. 5:2

*T*he place called "home" can be the most wonderful place on earth — or it can be a place of sheer misery.

I once preached in a state reformatory for boys — back before the American Civil Liberties Union and other such ungodly organizations decided that morality and Jesus Christ were unwelcome in government-run institutions.

A young fellow who had given his heart to the Lord at the end of my talk came up to see me. He told me, "My name will be changed legally in a few days, and I am so glad."

I asked him why that was so. He responded. "My mother and father are both alcoholics. Our home was a battleground. Today they are both in jail. They caused my delinquency. I intend to come out of this reformatory with a new name and start a new life without them."

I hardly knew how to answer the young man. I laid my hand on his shoulder and said, "God bless you as you leave this reformatory and may you never return again except to give thanks to these people for whatever kindness and guidance they gave you. I am glad you are starting a new life spiritually today and that you are starting a new life physically next week. It is my prayer that you will give your own children a godly home — and that it will be a source of joy to you and to them."

Just calling a house a home does not make it one. The home is a sacred institution, instituted by God as a place for the propagation of the human race. It was designed to be the first school of human instruction.

The home is the primary means by which society transmits from one generation to the next its values and standards of right and wrong.

I was born and reared in the old-fashioned South, where puritanical ideals were exalted, cherished, and rehearsed before children from the time of their infancy.

In that society, a woman was a lady — and was not insulted by such a courtesy as having a door opened for her. She was respected, protected, and provided for. A woman was equal to a man in dignity and responsibility. However, in every respect she was expected to be an example of femininity, goodness, and virtue.

In that society, one of the first things that a boy learned was to esteem girls.

When I was a schoolboy, my mother cautioned me that at all times I was to be the protector of my sister, who was a few years my junior. Sometimes my chivalry earned me a black eye or a bloody nose — but the message got out that nobody was allowed to bully Lester Sumrall's little sister.

In today's besieged society, things have changed — dramatically.

The First Family

The family has been a vital part of American society for 200 years. But thousands of years before that, Almighty God created both the family and the home for a good reason. He ordained marriage. It did not simply evolve. Nor was it engineered by academics standing around observing with notepads and video cameras.

What was the first family like? How could they possibly know how to raise children?

That's not a hard question. Go into the jungles, and you will see people who have never known any type of modern civilization. Yet, they know how to take care of their young.

Go to the animal kingdom. Bears and lions know how to take care of their cubs. There's an intuitive force inside of each creature to take care of that which it produces.

God gave Adam and Eve that ability.

Just having a gift from God doesn't mean that humans always live up to it. After all, Adam and Eve were designed to live forever. God warned them in Genesis 2:17 that if they disobeyed His command, then "you will surely die" — meaning their physical bodies.

The day they became rebellious against God and deliberately defied their Creator and ate the forbidden fruit, their physical bodies began dying. Of course, they did not fall apart immediately. In fact, Adam lived to be 930 years old, according to the Bible.

Adam and Eve did not immediately realize the results of their fall, except for the sudden realization that they were naked. They were ashamed, and God had to make them clothes.

What died on the day that he ate the forbidden fruit?

Adam's relationship with God. God never walked with him again.

When Adam was thrust out of the Garden of Eden, he had no further communion with the Almighty.

When man is born again and becomes part of the family of God, he again becomes a son or a daughter of God. At that point he is reinstated into the position Adam had before he fell in the Garden.

Ephesians 2:4-5 says, "God, who is rich in mercy, made us alive with Christ even when we were dead in transgressions. . . ."

When God put Adam and Eve in the Garden, He saw that they needed a home. He built within their deepest instincts, a yearning to have a home and a family.

Adam and Eve no doubt quarreled, maybe every day and maybe every hour. You can just imagine him telling her, "You are the woman who ate me out of house and home!"

She would say, "Well, you're the man, and you should have done something so that the serpent couldn't get to me."

That agitated spirit got into their sons and caused one to kill another.

Cain knelt over his brother, Abel, who was bleeding, and didn't know what to do. He had never seen a human bleed.

Then Abel died.

Cain secretly buried the body to conceal the death. In his terrible guilt, he finally realized what it means to transgress against God.

It wasn't until Cain slew Abel that the members of the first family learned the true meaning of death.

Today, families are dying all around us. Children are murdering children. Husbands are abusing their wives. Wives are committing adultery. Only God can breathe new life back into a family beaten to death by anger, jealousy, greed, and lust.

Poison in the Home

A happy home doesn't happen by accident. It takes hard work and sacrifice. It is created by a husband and wife who work at caring for one another and keeping their love for one another alive. They work at it every day.

A successful home is not marked with fear: fear that dad will abuse mom; fear that the police are coming; fear that the husband will be in jail soon; fear that one of the family will be killed.

These things create tension in a home. A happy home is a showcase for good behavior, integrity, and commitment. The alternative is a life filled with tension, quarrels, divorce, and hatred.

When a man gives himself over to drunkenness, he takes on the character of a destroyer. He uses abusive language and sometimes he becomes violent, hitting and knocking around his wife or his children.

Then when he arrives in divorce court, he says, "I don't know what caused all of this."

It's like clutching a rattlesnake to your breast. When the thing bites you, it does little good to plead, "Oh, my, I had no idea that it would do that."

Likewise when a viper sinks its fangs deep into the skin of your loved one and you watch them die, what are you going to say if you are the one who brought it into your house?

Pornography, gambling, drugs — all can poison a home.

If you allow your family to watch movies of unclothed people clutching each other in lust, then you are exposing your children to pornography — whether you choose to call it that or not. Such "entertainment" has no place in a Christian family.

Do you have friends who say there is nothing wrong with having a *Penthouse* or *Hustler* magazine around the house? I am sure you have heard of supposedly devout deacons who have a complete *Playboy* collection. They try to excuse themselves with the lie that they only buy those magazines for the articles — that they ignore the pin-ups.

When you bring that sort of trash into your home, you are inviting in the devil. You are opening the door to demonic influences over your children and over your marriage. Those kinds of magazines were founded by people immersed in lives of greed and lust.

A Christian family cannot learn anything from hedonistic philosophies that support an indecent lifestyle, except to run from it.

A happy home cannot be filled with greed, either. The Bible clearly says that the love of money is the root of all evil. Greed of money and possessions causes us to covet — breaking one of the original Ten Commandments. To covet is to lust after that which is not ours — to ache with yearning for possessions that God has not provided.

My friends, we are supposed to use things and love people, not the other way around. When we covet, we begin to love things and use people. That attitude in a home destroys relationships because it reduces humans to objects. It also reduces you to being a slave to your possessions.

How many times have you heard somebody say that they cannot visit their loved ones because they are afraid to leave their house unattended? They would rather neglect their daughter or grandchildren so they can stay home and love their TV and their jewelry and their antiques. They are slaves to their junk.

Keep covetousness, greed, and lust for success out of your home. There is nothing wrong with God-centered, God-given ambition. Remember, however, that the apostle Paul told us to remain content in whatever state the Lord places us.

Multi-billionaire John D. Rockefeller was asked how much money was enough. He smiled at his interviewer and answered: "Just a little bit more." That may be a clever answer, but that lust for more can only result in heartache.

To my mind, you can make a million dollars, but if you can't hold your family together, then you are a failure. You may be the smartest lawyer in town, but if you can't keep your marriage intact, you have accomplished nothing. The beginning of success is in the home.

You work on it from the day you are married. And you never stop until they hang a wreath on your door and carry you out feet-first to the tolling of church bells.

A Laughing Home

Humor is a medicine. It will cure your sorrows, misunderstandings, and depressions. It is very important in the home to have what I call a laughing home.

A family without humor is dead.

Parents must be willing to listen to the little funny things that the children say, and laugh with them. It takes away heaviness. The husband, if he hears something funny that day, ought to tell it to his wife, and both of them laugh together.

Humor can teach an idea or concept better than a three-hour lecture. You can't give philosophy to children — they're too young to understand high-minded ideas. But they can understand a funny story that makes a point and at the same time provides a good belly laugh.

Humor is a tonic for a family. Who enjoys being in a home where everyone has a long face and nothing is funny?

Lighten up. Don't take yourself or your kids so seriously. A lot of things that happen around the home are funny, and parents should permit good-natured humor — even when they may be the object of the laughter.

Humor is a healer, and we should not neglect to use it in our home. It may not be something that comes automatically — we may have to create it or plan to do it on purpose.

We had three boys, and they were full of mischief, so we had plenty of funny stories to make us laugh. I hold like a treasure in my heart the times that my wife and I laughed with our boys when they were small.

When you laugh with your family, your love is enlarged, and the door is thrown open for doing many other things together. Take time to enjoy your kids' funny stories.

It's a healthy condition when everybody can laugh. It's good medicine for the home.

Like a Wagon Wheel

The biblical truth is that God was, and is, and always will be the founder of the family.

He is high and holy and transcends all His creation both in glory and beauty. He alone is wise, righteous, and just. The Lord himself testifies to us in His Word that He is our only hope.

He has given us such a wondrous gift — marriage. He has protected it and constructed it carefully. Like a wedding band, there is no end to it. It is a sacred institution.

The family is like a mighty wheel that goes round and round.

The giant wheel of the home has a hub at the center — the heart of the wheel. Here, grease is needed, because without it, heat and friction build up, destroying the wheel and grinding it into powder. When that happens the wheel begins to wobble, then fall off, leaving it ruined and useless. When lubricated, however, the hub holds the wheel solidly in place.

Out from the hub, thin, flimsy-looking spokes hold a wheel together. None of them are strong enough by themselves to bear much weight, but together such spokes bore the burdens in our forefathers' old Conestoga wagons — the prairie schooners that carried families west.

The third part of the wheel is the rim — a

shield, usually made of metal that provides the rolling power. If the rim is bogged in mud, the spokes and hub cannot move forward. If the rim comes loose, the whole wheel falls apart.

These three parts — the hub, the spokes, and the rim — are one and form the wheel. They need each other to function. The same is true for the family.

The hub of the family wheel represents spiritual strength through God. It is the master control area. Within the hub is the Holy Spirit, which permits the family wheel to function.

The spokes reaching out from the hub are the various attributes such as personal habits and right relationships. One spoke represents sex in its proper function within the marriage relationship. Another spoke represents good stewardship where the money is shared and used properly. Other spokes represent integrity, trust, commitment, communication, humor, forgiveness, and spiritual growth.

Strong spokes are vital to the survival of a family.

Around the wheel is the rim, which is the covering of God's love that protects the family and holds it together.

With God's help, we must strengthen and reinvigorate our families so they can become the strong wheels that God intends.

How can we strenthen our families?

We must fight back in the joy of the Lord and in His strength, depending on Him daily. We must let Him be God. We must believe Him and His promises to us, such as His assurances to help us to live victoriously.

Romans 5:17 says that those who receive God's overflowing grace and His free gift of righteousness reign as kings in life through Jesus!

Today, however, evil crouches and lurks like an animal at our doors. It desires to have us and our families. Even so, the weapons of our warfare, according to 2 Corinthians 10:4-5, are not man made, but spiritual. They are a gift to you and me from the Father to pull down the devil's strongholds.

Our Only Hope

God's supernatural gift of marriage — the uniting of one man and one woman — was given for our benefit and enjoyment.

What a mystery that two persons, with two separate minds, two separate willpowers, and two separate sets of emotions can come together and break down their own willpower and their own desires in favor of one another. The two become one. As long as they flow in unity, their union is the happiest that a person can have on earth. There is no greater joy than that of a home where the two are one in Christ Jesus.

The mystery of marriage relies on mutual commitment. The husband and wife must be covenanted to each other, physically, emotionally, and certainly spiritually — united to resist the evil forces working to divide them.

For a marriage to succeed, there must be one other vital element: God reigning as Lord of our lives. In Isaiah 43:10-11 we read that we are to be His witnesses that there is no other god. He alone is our mighty hope.

Psalm 93:1-2 declares how He reigns clothed with majesty, girded with strength — our protector, the great founder of marriage, the One who blesses our families, who keeps us in His care, and who watches over us all.

God does not change, according to Malachi 3:6 and Hebrews 13:8. Eternal and unchangeable, He reigns over our lives — if we will let Him.

To this Almighty One, all the nations of this world are as nothing, counted by Him less than nothing and worthless, according to Isaiah 40:17. He is the King of Glory whose throne is built upon righteousness and justice.

He is grand and glorious, merciful and wonderful. He is the High and Lofty One who inhabits eternity, whose name is Holy (Isa. 57:15), and who reigns by His power forever! (Ps. 66:7).

How fortunate we are to have such a protector in these difficult and changing times. Amid the confusion, He is the protector of our homes and our only true source. He is the God of Abraham, Isaac, and Jacob; the God of the Bible. He is the God who became flesh and walked among us. He is the High King of the universe!

Lord of Your Family

The Scripture plainly declares in Psalm 24:1 that "The earth is the Lord's, and everything in it, the world and all who live in it. . . ." God says in

Psalm 50:12, more or less, "It's all mine."

Hallelujah!

Psalm 47:8 says that He reigns over the nations!

He also rules over the family — if we will let Him. We can choose to be subject to the kingdom of God and thus reap the bountiful blessings of His reign, such as redemption and eternal life. Or we can choose to live as rebellious sinners and reap the curses of it, such as condemnation, death, and eternal damnation.

God's rule exists whether we want to believe or not.

In Matthew 28:18, before the Lord gave the Great Commission, He uttered probably the most important statement He would make to the Church. Yet, it is the least talked about part of the Lord's commission. He said: "All authority in heaven and on earth has been given to me."

Do you realize what this means? Jesus has all authority and power in heaven.

But, He says, He has it on earth also!

He is the ruler of all — including the institution of the family, which He loves so.

The apostle Paul wrote, by the Spirit, that not only is Jesus the head of the Church, but that all things have been put under His feet, including all principalities and powers (Eph. 1 :20-22; Col. 2:10).

That's right!

No wonder Revelation 1:5 calls Jesus "the ruler of the kings of the earth." He is forever crowned the King of kings and the Lord of lords.

The truth is that God is Lord over the family, over our marriages, and over everything that we do.

We cannot trust in the ways of man. We must rest our hope firmly in the God who controls the universe.

We have a choice. We can choose to be governed by Almighty God as criminals and outcasts, or we can choose to believe on the Lord Jesus, repent of our sin, and be born anew as a subject of God's kingdom and joint heirs with Christ.

God is the undisputed, unchallenged, King of the family and the home and our marriages.

He reigns!

Let us commit our marriages and our homes to Him — declaring that He is Lord over everything. Diligently, daily we must seek His guidance and help. Faithfully, we must ask the Holy Spirit to help us to make our marriages work.

We must work to protect our homes and families — guided by and strengthened by our Lord.

In His love.

In His joy.

Seeking His help.

Praying for His protection, knowing that the family is His wonderful plan for you and me.